The Birth of the Modern

La Naissance de la Modernité

27. Florence H. McGillivray, *Venice*, 1918 (?) / *Venise*, 1918 (?)

The Birth of the Modern
La Naissance de la Modernité

Post-Impressionism in Canadian Art, c. 1900–1920

Le postimpressionnisme au Canada d'environ 1900 à 1920

Joan Murray

The Robert McLaughlin Gallery

Oshawa

Book design: Counterpunch / Linda Gustafson
Translation: Simone Auger, Elizabeth Schwaiger
Printing: TransContinental Printing

Murray, Joan, 1943–
The Birth of the Modern: Post-Impressionism in Canadian Art, c. 1900–1920

Catalogue of an exhibition held at The Robert McLaughlin Gallery, Oshawa, Ontario, November 1, 2001 to January 6, 2002; The Leonard and Bina Ellen Art Gallery, Concordia University, Montreal, Quebec, February 19 to March 30, 2002; Museum London, London, Ontario, August 3 to October 13, 2002; Beaverbrook Art Gallery, Fredericton, New Brunswick, November 24, 2002 to January 26, 2003; Winnipeg Art Gallery, Winnipeg, Manitoba, April 10, 2003 to June 29, 2003

ISBN: 0-921500-48-3

1. Artists, Canadian – 20th century – Exhibitions. 2. Art, Modern – 20th century – Canada – Exhibitions. 3. Painting, Canadian – 20th century – Exhibitions. 4. Post-impressionism (Art) – Canada – Exhibitions.
I. The Robert McLaughlin Gallery. II. Title

759.11

Conception graphique : Counterpunch / Linda Gustafson
Traduction : Simone Auger, Elizabeth Schwaiger
Imprimé et relié au Canada par Imprimeries Transcontinental

Murray, Joan, 1943–
La Naissance de la modernité: le postimpressionnisme au Canada d'environ 1900 à 1920

Catalogue d'une exposition à la Robert McLaughlin Gallery, Oshawa (Ontario), du 1er novembre au 6 janvier 2002; The Leonard and Bina Ellen Art Gallery, Université de Concordia, Montréal (Québec), du 19 février au 30 mars 2002; Museum London, London (Ontario), du 3 août au 13 octobre 2002; Beaverbrook Art Gallery, Fredericton (Nouveau-Brunswick), du 24 novembre 2002 au 26 janvier 2003; Winnipeg Art Gallery, Winnipeg (Manitoba), du 10 avril au 29 juin, 2003

ISBN: 0-921500-48-3

1. Artistes, canadiens – XXe siècle – expositions. 2. Art moderne – XXe siècle – Canada – expositions. 3. Peinture canadienne – XXe siècle – expositions.
4. Postimpressionnisme (arts visuels) – Canada – expositions.
I. The Robert McLaughlin Gallery. II. Titre

759.11

There was some excitement in London last month over the exhibition called the "Post- Impressionists." Everybody laughed and jeered but with a few exceptions it consisted of good things – art that will last.

James Wilson Morrice in a letter to Edmund Morris, 9 January 1911
Edmund Morris Letterbooks, E.P. Taylor Art Reference Library Archives,
Art Gallery of Ontario, Toronto.

I wanted now *to find out what this "New Art" was about. I heard it ridiculed, praised, liked, hated. Something in it stirred me, but I could not at first make head or tail of what it was about. I saw at once that it made recent conservative painting look flavourless, little, unconvincing.*

Emily Carr
On modern art in Paris in 1910
From her book *Growing Pains* (Toronto: Oxford, 1946), pp. 288–289.

If a man wants to paint a woman with green hair and red eyes he jolly well can.

William Brymner in conversation with students, among them painter Anne Savage, looking at a painting by John Lyman in the Spring exhibition at the Art Association of Montreal around 1913. Recounted by Anne McDougall, *Anne Savage: The Story of a Canadian Painter* (Montreal: Harvest House, 1977), p. 37.

Le mois dernier à Londres, une exposition intitulée « Les postimpressionnistes » a fait sensation. Elle a été l'objet de la risée universelle. Néanmoins, à part quelques exceptions, l'exposition contenait des bonnes choses – de l'art qui va durer.

James Wilson Morrice à Edmund Morris, 9 janvier 1911,
Edmund Morris Letterbooks, E. P. Taylor Art Reference Library,
Musée des beaux-arts de l'Ontario, Toronto.

J'ai voulu saisir sur le champ *la nature de cet « art nouveau ». J'entendais soit des remarques dérisoires, soit des éloges; on aimait, on détestait. Quelque chose dans cet art m'émouvait profondément, mais au début je n'arrivais pas à comprendre de quoi il retournait. J'ai vu tout de suite qu'en comparaison, la peinture conservatrice des années récentes était insipide, sans envergure, peu convaicante.*

Emily Carr : Remarques sur l'art moderne à Paris en 1910.
Extrait de sa biographie *Growing Pains*
(Toronto : Oxford, 1946), pp. 288–289.

Si un homme a envie de peindre une femme avec des cheveux verts et des yeux rouges, libre à lui!

William Brymner en conversation avec ses étudiants dont Anne Savage, devant un tableau de John Lyman au Salon de printemps de la Société des beaux-arts de Montréal, vers 1913. Cité dans Anne McDougall, *Anne Savage: The Story of a Canadian Painter* (Montréal : Harvest House, 1977), p. 37.

Contents

Table des matières

Preface

The era of Post-Impressionism in Canadian art is charged with the excitement of change and promise. The *modern* is truly born, and coincident with its arrival is a burgeoning confidence in a style that is genuinely identifiable as Canadian. The artists, especially the painters whose ideas and practices are contemporary with and consequent upon Impressionism, are not only concerned with finding their own individual voices within the explosion of possibilities but also with expressing a newly discovered sense of what can only be described as a national vision. No longer content to follow in the wake of the Europeans and Americans, the Canadians make Post-Impressionism their own idiom.

The particular strengths of the collection at The Robert McLaughlin Gallery have been developed in a coherent and intelligent way, informing our advantage in telling this part of the story of Canadian art. In no small way that strength is due to Joan Murray, director of the gallery for more than twenty-five years, and the curator for this exhibition. We are grateful to Joan, and I compliment her for her insightful catalogue as well as for organizing this unique opportunity to understand the work of those artists who gave birth to modernism in Canada. The exhibition and catalogue promise to be important contributions to our comprehension of early-twentieth-century Canadian painting in the way that Canadian responses to the Post-Impressionists are surveyed and vital links with modernism in both Europe and the United States are demonstrated.

The Robert McLaughlin Gallery, in its programs and its collection, has always had a special interest in that exhilarating period of Canadian art when imitation of European and American styles was relinquished for the enterprises and opportunities of modernism. This was the time when the Group of Seven arose, and with the complexity of other visions inspired by the modern, eventually saw such movements as Painters Eleven. The founding of the gallery and the earliest aims of its collection are identified with the heritage of this period.

The gallery is grateful to those institutions and private collectors whose loans to the exhibition have ensured its success. I also wish to give special thanks to Linda Jansma, curator, and Andrea Kelly, secretary, for their indispensable involvement in organizing the exhibition. As well, I'd like to extend sincere thanks to the Museums Assistance Program, Department of Canadian Heritage, for generous financial assistance.

David Aurandt
Executive Director
The Robert McLaughlin Gallery, Oshawa

Préface

Riche de promesse et de changement, le postimpressionnisme a été dans l'histoire de l'art canadien une période éminemment passionnante. C'est avec lui qu'est née la *modernité*, accompagnée d'une confiance grandissante en un style manifestement canadien. C'est à travers lui, et les multiples possibilités qu'il offrait, que nos artistes — particulièrement les peintres dont les idées et les méthodes relevaient ou dérivaient de l'impressionnisme – ont tenté non seulement de se trouver eux-mêmes, mais encore d'exprimer ce qu'on pourrait appeler une vision nationale. Ne se contentant plus de marcher dans les traces des Européens et des Américains, ces artistes se sont approprié le postimpressionnisme et en ont fait leur propre langage.

La Robert McLaughlin Gallery est bien placée pour relater cette phase de l'art canadien. En grande partie grâce à Joan Murray, sa directrice depuis plus de vingt-cinq ans et aussi la conservatrice de cette exposition, elle a su développer avec intelligence et cohérence sa collection postimpressionniste. Je tiens ici à exprimer notre reconnaissance commune à l'égard de Joan, et à la féliciter pour son catalogue pénétrant et pour son exposition qui nous permet de mieux saisir l'œuvre de ceux qui ont introduit la modernité en art canadien. En offrant une vue d'ensemble de la réponse des artistes du pays au postimpressionnisme, et en démontrant les attaches vitales qui relient leurs tableaux au modernisme européen et américain, son exposition et son catalogue sont appelés à former une contribution de taille à notre compréhension de la peinture canadienne du début du vingtième siècle.

Les programmes et la collection de la Robert McLaughlin Gallery témoignent de l'intérêt distinctif qu'entretient la galerie pour cette période stimulante de l'art canadien, marqué par le renoncement à l'imitation des styles européens et américains au profit de l'aventure excitante de la modernité. Cette époque a vu la naissance du Groupe des Sept, puis d'autres mouvements tels les Painters Eleven, la modernité ayant donné lieu à un ensemble complexe de visions diverses. La création de la galerie et les tout premiers buts de sa collection sont associés au patrimoine de cette période.

Nous remercions les institutions et les collectionneurs privés qui ont bien voulu prêter des tableaux à cette exposition et en assurer le succès. Des remerciements particuliers vont à Linda Jansma, conservatrice, et Andrea Kelly, secrétaire, pour leur indispensable collaboration dans l'organisation de cette exposition. Je souhaite également dire notre gratitude au Programme d'aide aux musées du ministère du Patrimoine canadien, pour sa généreuse assistance financière.

Le directeur général,
The Robert McLaughlin Gallery,
Oshawa,
David Aurandt

Introduction: Savage Work

Joan Murray

At the beginning of the twentieth century, Post-Impressionism was everywhere: from France, where it originated in 1886, to Italy; from Great Britain to Canada. Although the term *Post-Impressionism* was coined by the British art critic and painter Roger Fry in 1906, it is most commonly associated with a show he organized four years later at London's Grafton Galleries, titled *Manet and the Post-Impressionists*.[1] Yet, like many concepts invented by art critics, it still elicits a fair amount of confusion, even among art professionals.

When Fry used the term *Post-Impressionism*, he used it to designate a number of artists who viewed themselves as independent of Impressionism. In his 1910 exhibition, he gave examples of those artists he considered Post-Impressionist. Among his selections were Paul Cézanne, Vincent van Gogh, Paul Gauguin, Georges Seurat and Henri Matisse, as well as Symbolist artist Odilon Redon, among many others.

The artists grouped as Post-Impressionists display a variety of characteristics. Cézanne, who wished to make of Impressionism "something solid and enduring, like the art of the museums," analysed nature for its structure, producing an art concerned with the apprehension of volumes in space. Gauguin, however, was interested in cultures that he considered exotic and explored the symbolic use of colour and line. Van Gogh, the precursor of Expressionism, used dazzlingly intense colours, boldly handled. Clearly, the factor that united such artists was their desire to create a more expressive and individual kind of art, partly through bolder, abstracted forms, partly through decorative elements of line and composition, partly through the use of bright, sometimes arbitrary colour.

A typical example of Post-Impressionist painting from the period is Gauguin's *The Vision after the Sermon – Jacob Wrestling with the Angel* (1888). It was one of a group of paintings in which the artist applied a style incorporating flat areas of vivid colour and simple shapes to a subject he considered picturesquely primitive: the inhabitants and physical geography of Brittany on the west coast of France. In this painting the artist has depicted a scene in which the traditionally garbed Breton women have a vision of the subject that the priest had taken for a text in his sermon. In a letter to van Gogh, Gauguin wrote that the landscape existed only in the imagination of the people at prayer – thus, the lack of unified scale between the struggling figures and the people in the foreground. Like other Post-Impressionists, Gauguin believed the expression of his personal vision was more important than the mere representation of visual appearance.

Today, British writers like Bernard Denvir, author of the 1992 book *Post-Impressionism*, agree with Fry that the term *Post-Impressionism* applies to art made during a specific span of time,

extending from the end of Impressionism in 1886 with the Impressionist's eighth and last exhibition, to the introduction of Cubism towards the end of 1906 (in Canada, this occurred in the early 1920s). But besides indicating a temporal period, the term implies art made with a specific point of view, one that differed radically from Impressionism. Denvir, for instance, records the growing sense of dissatisfaction among both established masters and members of the younger generation with the ideals and artistic practices of the Impressionist group. Internal dissensions, a basic disagreement between the relative importance of line versus colour and dissension over places to exhibit led to disquiet, he writes. This was polarized by the emergence of a new figure with startling ideas – the painter and theoretician Georges Seurat. Seurat employed a "scientific" method to his use of colour, one based on principles related primarily to the perception of visual experience that he had discovered through reading the work of scientists like Eugène Chevreul. Chevreul had explored the notion of the juxtaposition of colours to obtain the vibrating quality of light seen in nature. Seurat began to explore the idea that juxtaposed dots of paint are visually mixed by the eye and fused by it into one solid colour, applying it to his art around 1882 in small panels, and by 1883 to 1884, in major paintings. The results had a profound effect on painters discontented with what they considered to be the arbitrary technique of Impressionism. Seurat's work offered a change from the out-of-doors approach Impressionists had used to record fleeting effects of light, shade and atmosphere, substituting instead a method that began first with the pictorial conception, then looked to nature. The idea quickly became popular. "Art is an abstraction. Derive it from nature as you dream in nature's presence, and think more about the act of creation than the outcome," Gauguin advised a painter in 1888.[2]

Adherents to Post-Impressionism, in Canada as elsewhere, were united by their use of new forms, techniques and subject matter, all used to express a varied reaction to Impressionism. The art they made was diverse. Consider, for instance, the four great pioneers who introduced Post-Impressionism into Canadian art – James Wilson Morrice, John Lyman, David Milne and Lawren Harris – along with other great talents like Tom Thomson and Emily Carr. An examination of Morrice's art suggests that during the early part of his career he admired Gauguin and Bonnard. Later he came under the influence of Matisse, as did Lyman who studied at Matisse's school (see Figure 1, p. 13). Milne also looked to Matisse as the master to emulate, particularly after Milne's participation in the Armory Show in New York in 1913 where he saw Matisse's *Red Studio*. By contrast, Harris looked to different masters, perhaps combining in his style memories of the work of van Gogh and exhibitions he had seen as a student in Berlin, along with references to the style of the Italian Post-Impressionist Giovanni Segantini. Influence also had come from a show of Scandinavian art he had seen in Buffalo in 1913. Thomson, who never travelled abroad, would have picked up what he knew from his painting peers and his reading. Carr's attitudes were shaped through study in France with different teachers. Of these, the most important for Carr was perhaps the British expatriate, Henry Phelan Gibb.

For all of these artists, the effect was the same – a new vitality and exuberance, a breadth of handling and pictorial freedom. Post-Impressionism opened the way to independence from

Figure 1: Matisse and his students in the Académie Matisse, Paris, 1909 (Matisse is seated centre; John Lyman is fourth from the left).
Matisse et ses étudiants à l'Académie Matisse, Paris, 1909 (Matisse est assis au centre; Lyman est le quatrième à partir de la gauche).

outworn convention. Out of this independence, Canada evolved its own interpretation of the new art, one that was simultaneously at home and slightly out-of-place in the evolution of world Post-Impressionism. It was an interpretation marked by a lyrical intensity and an attachment to nature in which the unique and sometimes savage physical environment of Canada was adapted to European painterly models.

It can be seen in the Canadian use of colour, for example. In Post-Impressionism, colour is often said to be used in a special way, as a carrier of meaning. The result is colour used to dynamic effect, high in key. If we look at the colour Lawren Harris used to paint foliage in *Autumn [Kempenfelt Bay, Lake Simcoe]*, for instance, we discover exactly this effect, created through the application of coral, pink, Indian red and lavender in strokes of varying sizes. The accumulative effect coalesces into a distinct experience of space and place, one Post-Impressionist in essence, but one with its own syntax.

Characteristics of Post-Impressionist painting as it was adopted by Canadian artists include formal simplification, along with the elimination of tonal modelling, incidental detailing and depth progression that followed strict rules of perspective. Tom Thomson's *The Pool*, for instance, toys with the viewer's

perception. At once two- and three-dimensional in effect, this strongly optical, almost square painting, with its boldly stroked areas of brilliant colour, looks like a backdrop for a typically Canadian setting. Here Thomson returned to a subject he had painted previously, transforming the scene with impeccable virtuosity and energy. Recalling the cheerful formalism of European artists like André Derain during his Fauve period, Thomson's painting is deft, witty and surprising.

Sometimes, of course, Canadian artists were slow to make up their minds over the new work. The gods might be Cézanne, van Gogh and other Post-Impressionists, but their work took a while to digest.[3] Morrice, for instance, in a letter to Canadian artist Edmund Morris from Paris in 1910, wrote of a fine show he had seen of Cézanne's paintings. "Fine work, almost criminally fine," he called it. "I once disliked some of his pictures but now I like them all."[4]

As in Europe, the first manifestations of Post-Impressionism in Canadian art began to emerge before it became a full-blown movement – with Morrice, around 1903, according to John O'Brian.[5]

Morrice was a founding member of The Canadian Art Club, a group of artists that encouraged a new attitude towards artistic expression involving a quest for a rugged, stylistic originality. The CAC was founded in Toronto in 1907 and held annual exhibitions from 1908 until 1915 when it disbanded. In its early shows, the paintings displayed were often restrained in colour and atmospheric. By 1912, however, with members like Ernest Lawson (a full member in 1911), William H. Clapp (a full member in 1913), and Marc Aurèle de Foy Suzor-Coté (a full member in 1914), the exhibitions were dominated by Impressionism, with landscape scenes assembled of strokes of paint that varied from thick flecks to dots, combined with short, small brush strokes and heavily built-up surfaces.

Working abroad in 1903, Morrice came in contact with Post-Impressionism first-hand. In his work of that year he began to substitute thin washes of paint for the impasto surface he had previously favoured and to use colour more boldly. His newly acquired stylistic courage suggests that he was strongly influenced by Post-Impressionist artists, most likely Gauguin, writes O'Brian.

John Lyman was a student of Henri Matisse at the Académie Matisse (an experience movingly recreated by Lyman in his remarks in the Appendix of this book). Like Morrice, he eschewed the prevalent Impressionist style for something more radical.

Lyman, who studied at the Académie Julian from 1908 to 1909, had been introduced to Leo, Gertrude and Michael Stein by his cousin, American painter Henry Lyman Sayens in 1909.[6] The Steins would have shown him the accumulation of paintings on the cluttered walls of their apartment, many of them by Cézanne, and also may have introduced him to Matisse. Towards the end of that summer, Lyman met the English painter Matthew Smith: together they decided to study with Matisse at his academy. Matisse's curriculum at his school was traditional – drawing from classical sculpture and the model – but his comments on art of the day, composition, colour theory, and on considering the role of the subject, combined with the example of his own work, changed Lyman's way of thinking about art.[7] Lyman's paintings of this date present a summary effect rather than detailed analysis, employing flattened form,

a generalized feeling for space, a thinly painted surface and strong, flat colours. Shown in Montreal in the Spring Exhibitions of the Art Association of Montreal from 1910 on, his work soon began to receive critical attention. In 1912, Lyman's painting, the Post-Impressionist movement and the lives of the founders were discussed in the Montreal *Gazette*, though the newspaper warned that such primitivism was "chill as death to art."[8]

By 1913, Post-Impressionism was coming to broad public consciousness in Canada. Interest was fed by several exhibitions that took place that year, all of them packed into that winter and spring: first came the International Exhibition of Modern Art (the so-called Armory Show) in New York, which included the work of Canadian Post-Impressionist artists David Milne and Middleton Manigault, followed by a two-person show of A.Y. Jackson and Randolph Hewton at the Art Association of Montreal, and finally the Art Association's Spring Show that included the work of Hewton, Jackson and Lyman. Still another show followed in Montreal in May – a five-year retrospective of Lyman's work at the Art Association.

Of the four shows, the Armory Show was by far the most important introduction to the birth of modern art. This huge concentration of late Impressionist, Post-Impressionist, Cubist and Futurist painting presented an impressive cross-stratum of the new art to the public. Along with work by North American artists, there were one hundred and twenty works by fifteen major French artists and one-person exhibitions of modern masters like Matisse. There was even a loan from Sir William Van Horne of Montreal, a canny collector who owned a handsome portrait of Cézanne's wife. Doubtless under the urging of the dealer from whom he had bought it – Stephen Bourgeois, who opened his business in Paris in 1906 – Van Horne lent it to the Armory Show.[9]

To a large extent, such shows challenged the taste of the art-viewing public. And given the revolutionary temper of the art, the reaction in the press was perhaps understandable. In Montreal, the Spring Show was reviewed with angry ferocity in the *Daily Witness* and by Samuel Morgan-Powell, the drama critic, in the *Daily Star*. The writer in the *Witness* began his article by describing the gasps of astonishment, indignation and derisive comment caused by the Post-Impressionists at the opening of the exhibition. "Immensity of canvas, screamingly discordant colors, and execrable drawing are the methods they have employed to jar the public eye," he wrote.[10] He continued at length in the same vein, criticizing the work of Hewton, Jackson and Lyman (he described the trees and water in Lyman's *Wild Nature* as displaying as much artistic skill as the well-known willow pattern on a plate) (see Figure 2, p. 25). But by his third column, he had conceded that the Post-Impressionists had a sense of mission, which he determined was to pay more attention to colour, vibration and impulse than to the mere reproduction of exterior form. Morgan-Powell was far more negative. He wrote that Post-Impressionism was a craze and that van Gogh and Gauguin were a couple of Montmartre cranks.[11] Lyman's *Wild Nature* he called a "daub of crude colours" with wretched drawing.

Among the many articles and letters to the press that followed was a feisty response from Lyman in which he quoted prices for Post-Impressionist works and defined Post-Impressionism, though not without a dig at the lack of sophistication of the Montreal critics. Post-Impressionism is a term, he

wrote, that has "only come into vogue since the first great exhibition of modern art in London... and serves, with mere chronological correctness, to denote that general art movement subsequent to Impressionism, which originated in France and has spread over all the civilized Occident."[12]

The vigorous discussion surrounding Post-Impressionism did not end with his letter to the editor, but continued with a criticism in the Montreal *Gazette* about Lyman's show in May. In this review, the writer found fault with Lyman's work of 1911 to 1913, pointing out its lifeless tones and disregard for form. Even his titles – Lyman often used the words *essay* or *impromptu* to describe his paintings – were criticized. So was his knowledge of anatomy.[13] Morgan-Powell rejoined the debate with an extraordinarily mean-spirited review. Now he described Lyman's work from 1911 on as "disastrous" and criticized a portrait of a model at the beach as a "disgusting, sensual, leering, hideous figure, devoid of grace, devoid of humanity, devoid of anything save offensiveness."[14]

An article in the *Witness* describes that Lyman reacted to the criticism of the Spring Show with much surprise and pain.[15] How much more must his feelings have been wounded by the sustained barrage of articles with comments like "Ugly women with still uglier limbs... lifeless figures, lifeless trees, and lifeless color... the pictures are like nothing in nature or art."[16] No doubt stung by the criticism, Lyman left the country soon after his solo show to travel abroad, not returning for fourteen years.

Morgan-Powell in the Montreal *Daily Star* continued the attack during the autumn of 1913. In a review, this time about a show at the Royal Canadian Academy, he again decried Post-Impressionism, calling it a "blustering spirit."[17] After this article, the controversy quieted down. Indeed, by 1918, the publication of an article by French painter Robert Mortier in the avant-garde Montreal review *Le Nigog* praising Cézanne for his individual approach to art, marks the beginning of a more sympathetic attitude in Canada towards modern art.[18] Yet the newspaper accounts, so boisterous and covering nearly a year, must have prompted many to want to see for themselves what Morgan-Powell described as "rough, splashy, meaningless, blatant, plastering and massing of unpleasant colors in weird landscapes."[19]

Artists would certainly have been among the curious. The key year for many Canadian artists in developing their work towards broader design and purer colour was 1913. It was in 1913, for instance, that Tom Thomson and J.E.H. MacDonald in Toronto began to establish the first solid links between their work and Post-Impressionism. Working as commercial artists, they likely knew about the movement from the prestigious British magazine *Studio* or from other publications – or had been informed about stylistic features by colleagues who had studied abroad. The new art would in time shape the artistic direction of artists' groups beginning to coalesce from 1914 on, such as the group that resulted in the Group of Seven, founded in Toronto in 1920, and the Beaver Hall Group in Montreal (a node of creativity jammed into a house at number 305 Beaver Hall), which was also founded in 1920.

For most artists in Canada, Post-Impressionism was received second-hand through books and magazines, and as a consequence tended to be decorative and illustrative. Some, however, responded to the new art in a more authentic way through first-hand experience. David Milne, for instance, was struck by Matisse's *Red Studio*, which he had seen briefly at the Armory

Show. Milne adopted Matisse's compositional device of structuring the painting around a single hue – in the case of the Matisse, the colour red (Milne even titled one of his own works *Red*). In many paintings of this period, Milne made a single predominant colour the unifying element.

Milne revealed the impact of *Red Studio* on his work in other ways. In paintings that he created in a series, Milne asserted a limited spatial effect (always an interior) using local colours for individual objects – often (as with the Matisse) representations of paintings. The general effect in these works of calm absorption also recalls Matisse, although Milne's works register a very different mood: his models do recline languidly on a bed, but they also sit on sofas or rockers, often reading books, something Matisse's models never seemed to do.

Milne's scenes often have a quality of being glimpsed in passing, as through an open door. Indeed, as he wrote later of a Matisse he admired, "A picture seen while walking past an open door might be grasped completely enough to be remembered for life – if it is a good enough picture."[20] For Milne, Matisse's *Red Studio* was just such a picture.

The result in Milne's work was the creation of a modern visual grammar of colour and form that, even today, in picture after picture, resists easy absorption. Milne's works of this period take time to sink in. The more we look at them, the more the details – a sliver of light or a picture hanging on a wall – begin to resonate. Milne, like Matisse before him, created an allegory of the senses. His paintings exist both as painted surfaces and descriptive representations of the artist's studio filled with objects of biographic significance.

In Matisse's painting, objects took on a special life. Although *Red Studio* is devoid of human presence, the female form was a recurring theme in Matisse's work. Milne, too, made frequent use of the model, at least at this moment in his work. And like Matisse, he treated the model with detachment, as part of the collection of objects and furnishings in the room. He was also fascinated, like Matisse, with describing the interior as a hermetically independent space. It was a theme he developed more fully in later work, perhaps still recalling the image of Matisse's *Red Studio*.

Milne's immediate assimilation of Post-Impressionism is unusual among Canadian artists, most of whom approached the new art with considerable caution. A.Y. Jackson, for example, was slow to abandon Impressionism. The artist, who had travelled to Europe in 1910 to 1913, said later that he returned with a knowledge of Post-Impressionism, particularly the more scientific analysis of colour employed by Seurat (Georges Seurat had developed his divisionist painting technique in 1885 to 1886 to more precisely depict colour and light).[21] But despite Jackson's claim that he was searching for something more substantial than the sketchlike technique of Impressionism, his paintings created in France and Italy display the dot or fleck facture of Impressionism. His work became distinctly Post-Impressionist only in 1916 when he served as a Canadian war artist. At this point, he left Impressionism behind for good. He wrote later that he attributed the change in style to the effect of the war: "The impressionist technique I had adopted in painting was now ineffective, for visual impressions were not enough."[22]

One problem with applying the term *Post-Impressionism* to Canadian art of the period is that there was generally a thin line between late Impressionism and Post-Impressionism. The subject of Impressionism in Canadian art was substantially covered

in 1995 by Carol Lowrey for the Americas Society Inc. art gallery in New York, in her exhibition *Visions of Light and Air: Canadian Impressionism, 1885–1920*. The show included many "borderline" artists and others who might more properly be called Post-Impressionists. I have tried to make the distinction clear here.

The term *savage* has often been used to describe Post-Impressionist painting. Morrice, for instance, in an often-quoted remark said about the work of Cézanne: "His is the savage work that one would expect to come from America."[23] One advantage of living in North America for artists touched by the Post-Impressionist impulse was that the environment lent itself to the new style.[24] Large parts of the countryside had a conspicuously desolate appearance (the meaning of "wild" according to the *Oxford Dictionary*). Canada's Group of Seven assimilated this concept into their work, creating "wild" landscape subjects very different from the settled farmland painted by John Lyman, for instance.

In his early work, however, even John Lyman drew on the concept of a uniquely Canadian wilderness – in his painting *Wild Nature (1), Dalesville* in which he drew specifically on pictorial ideas of Matisse. The work was only one among a host in the same period. The subject had great allure for artists at this time not only because of the influence of art from abroad, but also because of the Canadian public's interest in nature, led by a passionate group of naturalist artists such as Ernest Thompson Seton, nature poets such as Sir Charles G.D. Roberts, Bliss Carmen and Duncan Campbell Scott, as well as concerned naturalists. One of these naturalists was Dr. William Brodie, Tom Thomson's cousin, an important entomologist, ornithologist and botanist.

The influence of individuals like Brodie was widespread. They were committed to an essentially spiritual view of nature, a view shaped by their upbringing – often Scotch Presbyterian – and their immersion in the work of the American Transcendentalists, Ralph Waldo Emerson and Henry David Thoreau. In his essays, Emerson sought to recover man's original connection to the universe, enjoyed by earlier generations, who beheld God and nature face to face. Thoreau, his disciple and friend, the writer of *Walden*, went one step further in becoming the practising sage of the simple life.

The idea of spiritual and physical connection to nature as inspiration for an indigenous national art became a potent one for Canadian artists. However, as many of them quickly realized, it was not always necessary to travel great distances to paint Canadian nature. For instance, J.E.H. MacDonald, one of the founders of the Group of Seven, painted *The Tangled Garden* in 1916 from a sketch made in the garden of his home at Thornhill, near Toronto. This vivid, dynamic scene in which the artist offers a relaxed homage to the sunflowers of van Gogh summarizes Canadian art's outdoor roots, even if the out-of-doors in this case was a domestic garden.

An attachment to nature is not unique, of course, to Canada. Peter Morrin, who curated the ground-breaking *The Advent of Modernism: Post-Impressionism and North American Art, 1900–1918* exhibition in 1986 at the High Museum in Atlanta, wrote in his catalogue that Canada's Group of Seven was an art colony, one related to other artists' groups worldwide. Art colonies at Old Lyme in Connecticut, Worpswede in Germany and Nagybánya in Hungary all celebrated the unique beauty of their home environments.[25] In Canada, the idea had an especially long life.

Even today, Canadian artists celebrate a consciousness of nature in their work.

Griselda Pollock, in her slim but significant book *Avant-Garde Gambits 1888–1893: Gender and the Colour of Art History* (1993), has written about the extensive narrative in the work of Gauguin and related painters that combines tourism and modernism. In Canada, as in Europe, there was a dramatic increase in travel and tourism because of the expansion of the railway and the accelerated industrialization of the cities. Urban dwellers, Canadian artists among them, were eager to retreat to the countryside. The real Canadian innovation lay in incorporating a feeling of connection to "wild nature" and constructing a narrative around the concept of wilderness areas.

One of these wilderness areas was Algonquin Park, one hundred and forty kilometres north of Toronto, which was opened in 1893. In 1894, an Act of the Ontario Legislature established the area as one reserved and set apart as a public park and forest reservation, fish and game preserve, health resort and pleasure ground (the words are from the Act). This immense tract of land and water included and protected the headwaters of five major rivers that flow from the Park. It was regarded as a vast wilderness rich in possibilities – the playground, sanitarium and forest school for the future.[26] The creation of the Park fed a current of late-nineteenth-century nature worship stimulated most notably by the American author James Fenimore Cooper. Best known for his *Leather-Stocking Tales*, Cooper was read avidly throughout the nineteenth century. Shades of Cooper's image of the *forest primeval* linger in the words of one of the individuals who shaped the Act, Alexander Kirkwood. In his 1886 letter to T.B. Pardee, the Commissioner of Crown Lands, Kirkwood described the gloomy grandeur of the natural forest: "It is in wandering through such scenes that the mind drinks deep but quiet draughts of inspiration."[27]

Artists of the early twentieth century, like Canadian Victorian artists, found that nature offered a constant source of imagery. In May 1912, about the time *Saturday Night* magazine carried an article on "A Holiday in Algonquin Park," the artist Tom Thomson made his first visit there.[28] While he began to mine the imagery of the Park in his art, faraway in British Columbia Emily Carr was painting the artifacts of the First Nations people with empathy. In 1907, in Sitka, Alaska, she had resolved to record the totem poles of British Columbia, and from 1908 to 1912, she focused her attention on this extraordinarily ambitious project.

In their own ways, both Thomson and Carr helped invent our vision of Canada and particularly our idea of a natural world in opposition to the city. Sites like Algonquin Park and the villages of the indigenous peoples of British Columbia, because they were so recognizably Canadian and so finely observed in paint, inspired some of the country's most interesting Post-Impressionist work. Although the viewer may bring a variety of feelings to these subjects, the images are today an enduring part of a Canadian myth, a myth comparable to a religion, which has fundamentally formed the way in which we organize our leisure time.

In short, the influence of Post-Impressionism on Canadian art was extensive. The artists who produced Post-Impressionist work made a major conquest of a new territory and initiated radical and far-reaching change. Some of them offered the movement the stamp of their personality while others, cautious almost

to a fault, expressed its influence in their work without flamboyance. In reconciling local traditions with an international style, artists enlarged Canadian art, infusing it with new vitality.

Joan Murray
Director Emerita
The Robert McLaughlin Gallery, Oshawa

1. See Jacqueline V. Falkenheim, *Roger Fry and the Beginnings of Formalist Art Criticism* (Ann Arbor, Michigan: UMI Research Press, c. 1980), quoted in Richard R. Brettell, *Modern Art 1851–1929* (Oxford: Oxford University Press, 1999), p. 21.
2. Paul Gauguin to Emile Schuffenecker, Pont-Aven, 14 August 1888, in Françoise Cachin, *Gauguin: The Quest for Paradise* (London: Thames and Hudson, 1992), p. 176.
3. A.Y. Jackson wrote that Cézanne, van Gogh and other moderns were the gods of the Group of Seven. See Jackson to Catherine Breithaupt, Boston, 17 January 1921, Breithaupt Bennett papers, University of Waterloo Library, Waterloo, cited in Charles C. Hill, *The Group of Seven: Art for a Nation* (Ottawa: National Gallery of Canada, 1995), p. 24.
4. J.W. Morrice to Edmund Morris, 30 January 1910, Edmund Morris Letterbooks, E.P. Taylor Art Reference Library Archives, Art Gallery of Ontario, Toronto.
5. See John O'Brian, "Morrice's Pleasures (1900–1914)," in Nicole Cloutier et al., *James Wilson Morrice 1865–1924* (Montreal: Montreal Museum of Fine Arts, 1985), p. 93.
6. See Louise Dompierre, *John Lyman, 1886–1967* (Kingston: Agnes Etherington Art Centre, 1986), p. 29.
7. See Xavier Girard, *Matisse: The Wonder of Colour* (New York: Gallimard, 1994), pp. 58–60. It's not completely clear when Lyman attended Matisse's school. Girard records that the convent was sold in the summer of 1909 and the family moved into a residence on the outskirts of Paris. Yet, according to Louise Dompierre, Lyman most likely attended the school at the convent during the winter of 1910. (For the date of Lyman's attendance, see Louise Dompierre, *John Lyman, 1886–1967* [Kingston: Agnes Etherington Art Centre, 1986], p. 31). Lyman could have been there earlier since he appears fourth from the left in a photograph of Matisse among his students at the Académie Matisse (1909–1910), photograph Archives Matisse, Paris.
8. "Post Impressionism: Review of Movement Which Has Stirred Controversy," Montreal *Gazette*, 30 March 1912.
9. John Rewald, *Cézanne and America: Dealers, Collectors, Artists and Critics, 1891–1921* (Princeton: Princeton University Press), p. 173.
10. "Post-Impressionists Shock Local Art Lovers at the Spring Art Exhibition," Montreal *Daily Witness*, 26 March 1913.
11. S. Morgan-Powell, "Art and the Post-Impressionists," Montreal *Daily Star*, 29 March 1913.
12. John Lyman, "To the Editor: Mr. John G. Lyman Writes in Defence of 'Post-Impressionism,'" Montreal *Daily Star*, 1 May 1913.
13. "Pictures Will Revive Strife," Montreal *Gazette*, 21 May 1913.
14. S. Morgan-Powell, "Essays, Fugues, Adventures and Improvisations," Montreal *Daily Star*, 23 May 1913.
15. "More Post-Impressionism at the Art Gallery," Montreal *Daily Witness*, 21 May 1913.
16. Montreal *Daily Witness*, 21 May 1913.
17. S. Morgan-Powell, "A Few Notable Canvases, But a Lower Average," Montreal *Daily Star*, 23 November 1913.
18. Robert Mortier, *Le Nigog* 1, 4 (April 1918), pp. 119–120.
19. S. Morgan-Powell, Montreal *Daily Star*, 23 November 1913.
20. Quoted in David P. Silcox, *Painting Place: The Life and Work of David B.*

Milne (Toronto: University of Toronto Press, 1996), p. 387, note 23. I differ here from Silcox, who relates Milne's compositional device to Velazquez and Vermeer (p. 41).

21. Interview with A.Y. Jackson by the author, 4 March 1971. Joan Murray, Tom Thomson Papers.

22. A.Y. Jackson, *A Painter's Country: The Autobiography of A.Y. Jackson* (Toronto, Vancouver: Clarke, Irwin, 1958), p. 47.

23. Morrice to Morris, 30 January 1910.

24. I use the word *environment* in its largest, Marshall McLuhan-esque sense as meaning an active process that is invisible. See Marshall McLuhan with Quentin Fiore, *The Medium Is the Message: An Inventory of Effects* (New York: Bantam Books, 1967).

25. Peter Morrin, "An Overview: Post-Impressionism and North American Art," *The Advent of Modernism* (Atlanta: High Museum of Art, 1986), p. 15.

26. See, for instance, Thomas W. Gibson, "Algonquin National Park," *Canadian Magazine of Politics, Science, Art and Literature* (October 1894), p. 546.

27. A. Kirkwood, *Algonkin Forest and Park, Ontario: Letter to the Honourable T.B. Pardee, M.P.P., Commissioner of Crown Lands for Ontario* (Toronto: Warwick & Sons, 1886), p. 8.

28. "A Holiday in Algonquin Park," *Saturday Night*, 25 May 1912, pp. 4–5, 7.

Introduction : Un art sauvage

Joan Murray

Au début du vingtième siècle, le postimpressionnisme, qui avait vu le jour en France en 1886, s'était répandu de la France à l'Italie comme de la Grande-Bretagne au Canada : il était omniprésent. Inventé en 1906 par le critique d'art et peintre britannique Roger Fry, le terme *postimpressionnisme* n'a toutefois pris racine que lors de l'exposition *Manet and the Post-Impressionists* organisée quatre ans plus tard par Fry lui-même aux Grafton Galleries de Londres[1]. Semblable à beaucoup de concepts proposés par les critiques d'art, le mot prête encore aujourd'hui à confusion, même parmi les professionnels de l'art.

Quand Fry a employé le terme *postimpressionnisme*, il entendait désigner un certain nombre d'artistes qui s'étaient révoltés contre l'impressionnisme et se voulaient indépendants. Dans son exposition de 1910, Fry donne des exemples de ces peintres devenus à ses yeux postimpressionnistes : Paul Cézanne, Vincent Van Gogh, Paul Gauguin, Georges Seurat et Henri Matisse, ainsi que le symboliste Odilon Redon.

Les artistes regroupés sous l'étiquette du postimpressionnisme présentent des caractéristiques variées. Certains, tel Cézanne, avaient désiré faire de l'impressionnisme « quelque chose de solide et de durable, comme l'art des musées »; ils analysaient la nature pour en définir la structure, produisant un art soucieux d'appréhender les volumes dans l'espace. D'autres, tel Gauguin, intéressés aux cultures qui leur paraissaient exotiques, exploraient l'utilisation symbolique de la couleur et de la ligne, ou encore tel Van Gogh, le précurseur de l'expressionnisme, employaient des couleurs d'une intensité éblouissante maniées avec audace. Ce qui unissait clairement de tels artistes était leur désir de créer une forme d'art qui soit plus expressive et individuelle que l'impressionnisme, en utilisant divers moyens dont des formes abstraites plus hardies, des éléments décoratifs dans la ligne et la composition, et des couleurs éclatantes et arbitraires.

Ainsi Gauguin, dans *La Vision après le sermon – La lutte de Jacob avec l'Ange* (1888), l'un des chefs-d'œuvre du postimpressionnisme, a adopté un style fait d'aplats de couleurs vives et de simples formes pour rendre la Bretagne, sujet qui lui semblait primitif sur le plan pictural. Il a choisi de représenter ici des femmes bretonnes en costumes traditionnels ayant une vision du sujet apparemment traité par le prêtre dans son sermon. Dans une lettre à Van Gogh, il écrit que le paysage existait seulement dans l'imagination des fidèles – d'où le manque de proportions entre les combattants et les figurants du premier plan. À l'instar d'autres postimpressionnistes, Gauguin croyait que l'expression d'une vision personnelle était plus importante que la simple représentation d'un aspect visuel.

Aujourd'hui, des écrivains britanniques comme Bernard Denvir dans son livre *Post-Impressionism* (1992) sont d'accord

avec Fry pour voir dans le postimpressionnisme un art circonscrit dans une période donnée, débutant après l'impressionnisme, et allant de 1886 jusqu'à sa huitième et dernière exposition, puis se prolongeant jusqu'à l'arrivée du cubisme vers la fin de 1906 (au Canada, ceci s'est produit au début des années 1920). Mais en plus de se référer à une période spécifique, le terme implique un art au contenu particulier, radicalement différent de l'impressionnisme. Denvir, par exemple, fait état de la dissatisfaction croissante observée chez les maîtres reconnus et la génération montante face aux idéaux et aux pratiques du groupe impressionniste. Des dissensions internes, une dichotomie fondamentale entre la ligne et la couleur, et un désaccord quant au choix de lieux d'exposition ont abouti à une inquiétude polarisée par l'émergence d'un nouveau peintre et théoricien aux idées étonnantes : Georges Seurat. Seurat utilisait une méthode « scientifique » pour manier la couleur, basée sur un changement lié avant tout à la perception de l'expérience visuelle, et qu'il avait découverte en lisant l'œuvre de scientifiques comme Eugène Chevreul. Chevreul avait examiné la notion de juxtaposition des couleurs pour obtenir la qualité vibratoire de la lumière telle que perçue dans la nature. Aux environs de 1882, dans de petits tableaux, puis en 1883 et en 1884, dans d'importantes toiles, Seurat a commencé d'explorer l'idée que l'œil peut mélanger activement de petites touches séparées de peinture pour les fusionner en une seule et même couleur. Les résultats obtenus ont eu un effet profond sur les peintres mécontents de ce qu'ils considéraient comme la technique arbitraire de l'impressionnisme. À l'approche impressionniste qui exigeait que l'on peigne en plein air pour enregistrer les effets changeants de la lumière, de l'ombre et de l'atmosphère, Seurat proposait de substituer une pratique qui accordait la primauté à la conception picturale, quitte à ce qu'on se tourne ensuite vers la nature. L'idée a vite gagné en popularité. « L'art est une abstraction », observait Gauguin à un peintre en 1888[2]. Et de lui conseiller : « Faites-le dériver de la nature comme vous rêvez en présence de la nature, et pensez davantage à l'acte de créer qu'à son résultat. »

Au Canada comme ailleurs, l'emploi de nouveaux motifs, formes et techniques unissait les adeptes du postimpressionnisme, qui entendaient ainsi protester contre l'impressionnisme. L'art de ces artistes était cependant diversifié. Il n'est que de voir les œuvres des quatre grands pionniers du postimpressionnisme au Canada : James Wilson Morrice, John Lyman, David Milne et Lawren Harris, ainsi que de peintres aussi doués que Tom Thomson et Emily Carr. L'art de Morrice laisse croire qu'au début de sa carrière il admirait Gauguin et Bonnard. Il a subi plus tard l'influence de Matisse, tout comme Lyman, qui a étudié à l'Académie Matisse. Milne voyait aussi en Matisse le maître à émuler, surtout après sa participation en 1913 à l'Armory Show de New York où il aurait vu *L'Atelier rouge* de Matisse. Par contre, Harris admirait différents maîtres, et son style est peut-être un amalgame de plusieurs influences : de Van Gogh et d'autres peintres présentés à des expositions qu'il aurait visitées lors de ses études à Berlin; du postimpressionniste italien Giovanni Segantini; et de l'art scandinave qu'il avait découvert lors d'une exposition à Buffalo en 1913. Thomson, qui n'avait jamais voyagé à l'étranger, aurait tiré son savoir de ses lectures et de ses collègues, et Carr l'aurait obtenu de ses études en France sous différents professeurs et, plus encore, de l'expatrié britannique Henry Phelan Gibb.

Pour tous ces artistes l'effet était le même – une nouvelle vitalité exubérante, un affranchissement du geste et une liberté

picturale. Le postimpressionnisme marquait le premier jalon sur la voie de la libération de conventions désuètes.

Non que le Canada n'ait eu sa propre interprétation du postimpressionnisme, ce courant dans lequel il paraît à l'aise sans toutefois totalement s'y intégrer. Un lyrisme intense et un attachement à la nature caractérisent le postimpressionnisme canadien, tout en le situant dans un secteur de l'art mondial sensible à l'environnement. Son don particulier réside dans sa façon d'enflammer l'imagination au moyen de lieux indigènes – étrangement attirants aux yeux de certains plasticiens – et de procédés stylistiques glanés chez divers maîtres européens pour créer des orchestrations picturales complexes de couleurs, de formes et de lumière.

Prenons la couleur canadienne. C'est un truisme de dire que la couleur dans le postimpressionnisme est utilisée de manière spéciale, qu'elle est porteuse de sens, qu'on l'emploie de façon à créer un effet hautement dynamique. Ainsi, si l'on regarde la couleur qu'a utilisée Lawren Harris pour le feuillage de son tableau *Automne [Baie Kempenfelt, Lac Simcoe]*, on découvre des tons de corail, de rose, de rouge indien et de lavende appliqués en traits de grandeurs diverses, et qui se fondent pour donner lieu à une expérience distincte de l'espace et du lieu.

D'autres caractéristiques du postimpressionnisme incluent la simplification formelle, qui élimine le modelage des tons, les détails accessoires, et la progression en profondeur suivant les règles strictes de la perspective. *The Pool* de Tom Thomson, par exemple, joue avec la perception du spectateur. À la fois bidimensionnel et tridimensionnel, ce tableau fortement optique, presque carré, consistant en une suite de zones de peinture éclatante appliquée avec force, ressemble à une toile de fond pour une scène typiquement canadienne. Le peintre a transformé un sujet qu'il avait déjà traité en le peignant ici avec énergie et une impeccable virtuosité. Tout en évoquant le formalisme enjoué d'artistes européens comme André Derain durant sa période fauve, cette toile démontre que Thomson pouvait aussi être habile, spirituel et surprenant.

Parfois, bien sûr, les artistes canadiens étaient lents à se faire une opinion du nouveau langage pictural. Les dieux peuvent être Cézanne, Van Gogh et d'autres postimpressionnistes, mais il faut du temps pour absorber leur œuvre[3]. Ainsi, Morrice, dans une lettre qu'il envoyait de Paris en 1910 à l'artiste canadien Edmond Morris, raconte qu'il a vu une belle exposition de Cézanne. « Beau travail, dit-il, presque criminellement beau. » Et d'ajouter : « J'ai jadis détesté certaines de ses peintures, mais maintenant je les aime toutes[4]. »

Tout comme en Europe, le postimpressionnisme au Canada s'est fait jour longtemps avant la naissance du terme – avec Morrice, vers 1903, selon John O'Brian[5].

Morrice était l'un des membres fondateurs du Canadian Art Club, qui préconisait chez les artistes une nouvelle attitude face à l'art, les encourageant à rechercher une originalité stylistique vigoureuse. Fondé à Toronto en 1907, le Club a tenu des expositions annuelles de 1908 jusqu'à sa dissolution en 1915. Au début, les tableaux exposés étaient des œuvres d'atmosphère aux tons modérés, mais à partir de 1912, avec des peintres tels qu'Ernest Lawson (devenu membre en 1911), William H. Clapp (devenu membre en 1913), et Marc-Aurèle de Foy Suzor-Côté (devenu membre en 1914), la teneur des expositions est devenue principalement impressionniste – une sorte de tectonique de plaques picturale composée de motifs paysagers et de traits de pinceau

allant de taches épaisses à de simples points, que leurs auteurs combinaient avec des petits coups de brosse et des surfaces empâtées.

Alors qu'il travaillait à l'étranger, Morrice avait acquis une connaissance directe du postimpressionnisme et, en 1903, il avait commencé de remplacer l'empâtement qu'il privilégiait jusque-là par de minces couches de peinture et des couleurs plus vives. Son nouveau courage stylistique laisse croire à O'Brian qu'il a été fortement influencé par les postimpressionnistes, peut-être surtout par Gauguin.

Telle celle de Morrice, la peinture de John Lyman (qui avait étudié avec Henri Matisse à l'Académie Matisse comme le démontre son émouvant témoignage sur le maître français dans l'appendice) était beaucoup plus radicale (Figure 1, p. 13).

Lyman, qui avait aussi étudié à l'Académie Julian de 1908 à 1909, avait eu la chance d'être présenté en 1909 par son cousin, le peintre américain Henry Lyman Sayens[6], à Leo, Gertrude et Michael Stein. Les Stein lui auraient certainement montré les tableaux qui tapissaient les murs de leur appartement, dont plusieurs étaient de Cézanne, et l'auraient sans doute éventuellement présenté à Matisse. Vers la fin de l'été en cause, Lyman a rencontré le peintre anglais Matthew Smith, et ensemble ils ont décidé de s'inscrire à l'Académie Matisse. Le programme d'études y était traditionnel – dessin à partir de la sculpture classique et d'un modèle – mais les commentaires de Matisse sur l'art du jour, la composition, la théorie de la couleur et la vue d'ensemble d'un sujet ont modifié l'approche artistique de Lyman[7]. L'œuvre du Lyman de cette époque propose une vue synthétique d'un motif plutôt qu'une analyse détaillée, des formes aplaties, un sentiment d'espace, une surface mincement peinte, et des couleurs plates et fortes. Exposée à partir de 1910 aux expositions de printemps de l'Art Association of Montreal, sa peinture a attiré l'attention de la critique. En 1912, un article de la *Gazette* de Montréal discutait tout ensemble l'œuvre de Lyman, le terme « postimpressionniste », les buts de l'école et la vie des fondateurs, en déclarant toutefois qu'un tel primitivisme jetait sur l'art « un froid de mort »[8].

Figure 2: John Lyman, *Wild Nature / Nature sauvage (1), Dalesville*, 1912.

En 1913, le public canadien avait commencé de prendre conscience du postimpressionnisme. Plusieurs expositions avaient eu lieu tout au long de l'hiver et du printemps : d'abord l'International Exhibition of Modern Art (appelée l'Armory Show) à New York, qui incluait l'œuvre des postimpression-

nistes canadiens David Milne et Middleton Manigault; puis l'exposition des tableaux d'A.Y. Jackson et de Randolph Hewton à l'Art Association of Montreal; et enfin l'Exposition de printemps de l'Art Association qui comprenait des peintures de Hewton, Jackson et Lyman. Une autre exposition devait suivre en mai à Montréal – une rétrospective de cinq ans de l'œuvre de Lyman à l'Art Association. On doit surtout à l'Armory Show l'initiation du public à la naissance de l'art moderne. En effet, par son énorme concentration de tableaux néo-impressionnistes, postimpressionnistes, cubistes et futuristes, il offrait un vaste échantillon du nouvel art. Les œuvres d'artistes nord-américains voisinaient avec cent vingt tableaux de quinze peintres français de premier plan et des expositions solo de maîtres modernes comme Matisse. On y trouvait même un prêt d'un collectionneur canadien, Sir William Van Horne de Montréal, qui possédait un beau portrait de la femme de Cézanne; il l'avait sans doute prêté à l'Armory Show[9] à l'instigation du marchand qui le lui avait vendu, Stephen Bourgeois qui avait ouvert son commerce à Paris en 1906.

Ces expositions représentaient un cours d'éducation publique. Néanmoins, le caractère révolutionnaire de l'art a donné lieu dans la presse à des critiques négatives, bien que compréhensibles. À Montréal, l'Exposition du printemps s'est attiré un article d'une colère féroce dans le *Daily Witness* et un autre également vicieux du critique dramatique Samuel Morgan-Powell dans le *Daily Star*. L'article du *Witness* décrit d'abord les exclamations d'étonnement et d'indignation entendues lors du vernissage ainsi que les commentaires dérisifs occasionnés par les tableaux postimpressionnistes. Puis, l'auteur ajoute : « Une toile immense, des couleurs affreusement discordantes, et un dessin exécrable sont les méthodes employées pour secouer le public. »[10]. Il continue dans la même veine, critiquant longuement l'œuvre de Hewton, Jackson et Lyman (les arbres et l'eau dans *Nature sauvage* de Lyman, aujourd'hui un classique du mouvement, lui paraissent aussi artistiques que le motif populaire du saule sur une assiette; Figure 2, p. 25). Mais dans la troisième colonne de son texte, il se fait plus conciliateur, et concède que les postimpressionnistes se voient imbus d'une mission, qui consiste à accorder plus d'attention à la couleur, à la vibration et à l'impulsion qu'à la simple reproduction d'une forme extérieure. Morgan-Powell est beaucoup plus négatif. Le postimpressionnisme est pour lui un moment de folie, et Van Gogh et Gauguin lui semblent des excentriques de Montmartre[11]. Il va jusqu'à qualifier la toile *Nature sauvage* de Lyman de « barbouillage de couleurs crues » au dessin abominable.

Parmi les nombreux articles et lettres à l'éditeur qui s'ensuivirent, on note une réponse fringante de Lyman dans laquelle il cite le prix des œuvres postimpressionnistes, définit le postimpressionnisme, et laisse voir son mépris pour la réception qui lui a été accordée à Montréal (il utilise le mot « civilisé » d'une façon qui en dit long). L'impressionnisme, écrit-il, est une terme « entré en vogue seulement après la première grande exposition d'art moderne à Londres... et qui sert, pour les besoins de l'exactitude chronologique, à indiquer un mouvement artistique général, subséquent à l'impressionnisme, né en France et qui s'est propagé à travers tout l'Occident civilisé[12]. »

La lettre de Lyman à l'éditeur n'a pas mis fin pour autant à la discussion vigoureuse sur le postimpressionnisme. Au contraire, celle-ci s'est poursuivie dans la *Gazette* de Montréal à la suite de l'exposition de Lyman au mois de mai. Selon l'auteur du compte-

rendu, l'œuvre réalisée par Lyman de 1911 à 1913 est peinte dans les mêmes tons sans vie et démontre le même mépris de la forme. Même les titres des toiles n'échappent pas à sa critique (Lyman utilisait souvent le mot « Essai » ou « Impromptu » pour décrire ses tableaux). Et il en va ainsi des connaissances anatomiques du peintre[13]. Comme précédemment, Morgan-Powell s'est joint au débat en faisant une critique remarquablement mesquine. Les toiles de Lyman à partir de 1911 lui paraissent « désastreuses », et un portrait d'un modèle à la plage est pour lui « un personnage dégoûtant, sensuel, concupiscent, hideux, sans grâce, sans humanité, sans quoi que ce soit sauf la capacité de choquer[14]. »

Un article paru dans le *Witness* note que la critique de l'Exposition du printemps a beaucoup étonné Lyman et qu'elle l'a bien aussi un peu blessé[15]. On peut imaginer combien l'artiste a pu être meurtri par le flot soutenu d'articles contenant des commentaires tels que : « Des femmes laides avec des membres encore plus laids... des personnages sans vie, des arbres sans vie, de la couleur sans vie... ses tableaux ne ressemblent à rien dans la nature ni dans l'art[16]. » Sans aucun doute de telles critiques ont contribué à son départ pour l'étranger peu après son exposition solo et à son absence longue de quatorze ans.

Morgan-Powell a poursuivi son attaque dans le *Daily Star* de Montréal durant l'automne de 1913. Dans sa critique d'une exposition de l'Académie royale des arts du Canada, il dénonce de nouveau le postimpressionnisme, dans lequel il ne voit que « fanfaronnades [17]. » Après cet article, la controverse s'est calmée. En fait, en 1918, la publication d'un article du peintre français Robert Mortier dans la revue montréalaise d'avant-garde *Le Nigog*, qui loue l'approche artistique individuelle de Cézanne, indique qu'une attitude plus sympathique à l'égard de l'art moderne existe déjà au Canada[18]. Les critiques violentes des journaux parues pendant environ un an ont dû pousser plus d'un lecteur à vouloir se former une opinion indépendante et à aller voir les œuvres que Morgan-Powell qualifiait de « brutales, voyantes, dépourvues de sens, criardes, plâtrant et massant des couleurs désagréables sur de bizarres paysages[19]. »

Au nombre de ces spectateurs, il devait se trouver des artistes. En tout cas, l'année 1913 marque dans l'art de plusieurs peintres canadiens le début d'une évolution vers un dessin plus large et une couleur plus pure. C'est en 1913, par exemple, que les premiers liens solides avec le postimpressionnisme apparaissent dans les toiles de Tom Thomson et J.E.H. MacDonald. L'un et l'autre travaillaient en art publicitaire à Toronto, et devaient évidemment avoir lu sur le mouvement dans la prestigieuse publication britannique *Studio* ou dans d'autres revues. Des collègues qui avaient étudié à l'étranger ont pu aussi les tenir au courant des caractéristiques stylistiques du nouvel art. Cet art devait éventuellement constituer une partie du credo des groupes d'artistes qui ont commencé à se former à partir de 1914 – entre autres, celui qui allait donner naissance au Groupe des Sept fondé à Toronto en 1920, et cet autre, fondé aussi en 1920 mais à Montréal : le Groupe de Beaver Hall, ainsi nommé parce que le noyau créateur d'artistes qui le composait était entassé dans une maison sise au 305 Beaver Hall.

Inévitablement, l'art canadien qui suivait de près le postimpressionnisme – mais au travers de livres ou de revues – est devenu surtout un art de décoration et d'illustration, bien qu'à l'occasion un artiste ait pu adopter le postimpressionnisme européen de la toute dernière heure. Ainsi, David Milne a été influencé par *L'Atelier rouge* de Matisse, qu'il n'avait vu pourtant

que très brièvement à l'Armory Show. L'image-clé qu'avait retenue Milne de cette toile était sa dépendance d'une seule couleur – le rouge en l'occurrence, sur lequel seules ressortaient d'autres œuvres de Matisse. Milne a même intitulé un tableau « Red », et dans plusieurs de ses peintures de cette époque, une seule couleur prédominante sert de force agissante.

L'effet de *L'Atelier rouge* se fait sentir d'autres manières chez Milne. Milne revendiquait un effet spatial limité (toujours un intérieur) et des couleurs locales pour des objets individuels (eux-mêmes des tableaux comme chez Matisse). L'effet d'ensemble en est un de calme qui rappelle Matisse, bien que l'œuvre de Milne diffère grandement de celle de Matisse quant aux positions représentées : si, comme chez Matisse, ses modèles féminins sont parfois étendus langoureusement sur un lit, ses femmes sont également montrées assises sur un divan ou une berceuse, et souvent en train de lire un livre, ce que ne fait jamais un modèle de Matisse.

Milne a aussi rendu hommage à Matisse dans les scènes qu'il a peintes, plusieurs étant des intérieurs apercus au passage d'une porte ouverte, comme ceux de Matisse qu'il avait tant admirés comme il devait le rapporter plus tard. « On pourrait si bien s'être imprégné d'un tableau aperçu au travers d'une porte ouverte qu'on s'en souviendrait pour la vie – s'il est suffisamment bon », a t-il écrit[20]. *L'Atelier rouge* de Matisse était pour Milne un tel tableau.

Il en est résulté chez Milne une grammaire picturale moderne de couleurs et de formes, qui n'est pas facile d'accès. Il faut du temps pour comprendre le Milne de cette période. Plus on regarde ses peintures, plus se mettent à résonner en nous certains détails tels un rayon de lumière ou un tableau suspendu au mur. À l'instar de Matisse, Milne a créé une allégorie sensuelle. Ses toiles existent à la fois en tant que surfaces peintes et en tant que représentations du studio de l'artiste rempli d'objets munis de sens biographique.

Les objets chez Matisse ont une vie bien à eux : c'est là l'essence de sa peinture. Même si dans *L'Atelier rouge*, il n'y a pas de modèle dans la pièce, la forme féminine est un sujet qui revient souvent dans l'œuvre de Matisse. Milne aussi se servait fréquemment d'un modèle, du moins durant cette phase de sa carrière. Milne le traite avec détachement, comme s'il faisait partie de la pièce, comme le faisait Matisse quand il peignait sur modèle. Et comme Matisse encore, Milne se fascinait pour l'intérieur vu en tant qu'espace hermétique et autonome. C'est là un thème qu'il a développé à fond plus tard, se souvenant peut-être encore de la peinture de Matisse.

Contrairement à la plupart des artistes canadiens qui abordaient prudemment le postimpressionnisme, il a suffi à Milne d'un coup d'œil pour s'y plonger. Ainsi, A.Y. Jackson disait avoir rapporté d'Europe, où il avait vécu aux environs de 1910 à 1913, une connaissance du postimpressionnisme, en particulier de l'analyse plus scientifique de la couleur préconisée par Seurat; ce dernier avait développé de 1885 à 1886 une technique divisionniste pour rendre la couleur et la lumière avec plus de précision[21]. Cependant, même si Jackson disait chercher une technique de peinture plus substantielle que celle de l'impressionnisme, où tout devait paraître comme esquissé, les tableaux qu'il a peints en France et en Italie révèlent une structure de points et de petites taches caractéristiques de l'impressionnisme. Jackson n'est devenu postimpressionniste qu'en 1916, alors qu'il travaillait comme artiste de guerre canadien. Il a alors renoncé pour de

bon à l'impressionnisme. Il a écrit plus tard qu'il attribuait son changement de style à l'influence de la guerre : « La technique impressionniste que j'avais adoptée pour peindre était devenue inefficace, car les impressions visuelles ne suffisaient pas[22]. »

L'emploi, en art canadien, du terme *postimpressionnisme* peut faire problème vu la fine ligne de démarcation qui existe dans l'œuvre de certains artistes entre le néo-impressionnisme et le postimpressionnisme. L'exposition montée par Carol Lowrey, *Visions of Light and Air: Canadian Impressionism, 1885–1920*, et présentée à l'Americas Society Inc. art gallery à New York en 1995, donne une vue substantielle de l'impressionnisme canadien. L'exposition comprenait plusieurs artistes qui pouvaient à la rigueur être considérés comme impressionnistes et d'autres qui étaient plutôt postimpressionnistes. J'ai essayé ici d'établir entre les deux une distinction qui soit claire.

Le mot « sauvage » a souvent été associé à la peinture postimpressionniste. Ainsi Morrice a caractérisé l'œuvre de Cézanne par cette phrase souvent citée: « On se serait attendu à ce qu'une œuvre aussi sauvage provienne de l'Amérique[23]. » Au moins, les artistes nord-américains qui ont adopté le postimpressionnisme avaient cet avantage que le nouveau style convenait à leur environnement[24]. De vastes parties de la nature étaient manifestement désertes (en anglais « desolate », le sens même de « sauvage » selon le dictionnaire Oxford. Le Larousse français donne aussi ce sens au mot « désert »). Les membres du Groupe des Sept ont eu beau jeu d'appliquer le concept du postimpressionnisme dans leur œuvre et de créer des images « sauvages » à partir de paysages « sauvages », tout à fait différents des paysages européens, et à l'occasion toutefois, comme John Lyman l'a fait dans ses tableaux, à partir de payages représentant une nature apprivoisée.

Cependant, même John Lyman s'est laissé inspirer par le paysage sauvage typiquement canadien comme dans *Nature sauvage (1), Dalesville* où il applique certaines des idées picturales de Matisse. Ce tableau n'est qu'un exemple parmi tant d'autres réalisés à l'époque sur le thème de l'environnement canadien. Le sujet a captivé les artistes de la période non seulement à cause de l'influence de l'art d'outre-mer, mais aussi à cause d'un intérêt pour la nature chez le public canadien, intérêt entretenu par un groupe passionné d'artistes naturalistes comme Ernest Thompson Seton, de poètes de la nature comme Sir Charles G.D. Roberts, Bliss Carmen et Duncan Campbell Scott, et de scientifiques concernés. Parmi ces derniers, se trouvait le D^r^ William Brodie, un cousin de Tom Thomson et un important entomologue, ornithologue et botaniste.

Des gens tels que Brodie exerçaient une vaste influence. Ils avaient une vision essentiellement spirituelle de la nature, acquise durant leur éducation – souvent écossaire et presbytérienne – et renforçée par leur fréquentation assidue des écrits des transcendantalistes américains, Ralph Waldo Emerson et Henry David Thoreau. Emerson voulait retrouver le rapport originel à l'univers, dont avaient bénéficié les générations antérieures qui contemplaient Dieu et la nature face à face. Thoreau, son disciple et son ami ainsi que l'auteur de *Walden*, a même fait un pas de plus en allant vivre dans les bois.

À cette époque, vivre dans la nature était devenu un rêve pour plusieurs artistes canadiens, et même une réalité pour quelques privilégiés. Toutefois, comme plusieurs l'ont vite réalisé, il n'était pas toujours nécessaire de franchir de grandes distances pour peindre la nature canadienne. J.E.H. MacDonald, par exemple, l'un des fondateurs du Groupe des Sept, a peint *Le*

Jardin emmêlé en 1916 à partir d'un croquis dessiné dans le jardin de sa maison à Thornhill, près de Toronto. Ce tableau aux couleurs vives et à la composition dynamique, dans lequel l'artiste rend un hommage décontracté aux tournesols de Van Gogh, synthétise les racines de l'art canadien réalisé en plein air, même si le plein air en ce cas n'était qu'un jardin de banlieue.

L'attachement à la nature n'est pas l'apanage des seuls artistes canadiens. Comme Peter Morrin l'a écrit dans le catalogue de l'exposition révolutionnaire qu'il a montée en 1986 au High Museum d'Atlanta, *The Advent of Modernism: Post-Impressionism and North American Art, 1900-1918*, le Groupe des Sept était une colonie artistique semblable à d'autres colonies artistiques à travers le monde. Que ces colonies se trouvent à Old Lyme au Connecticut, à Worpswede en Allemagne, à Nagybánya en Hongrie, ou encore au Canada comme le Groupe des Sept, elles célébraient toutes la beauté unique de leur environnement[25]. Mais au Canada la chose a fait long feu. Même encore aujourd'hui, les plasticiens canadiens honorent dans leur art la conscience qu'ils ont de la nature.

Dans une mince mais importante étude, *Avant-Garde Gambits 1888–1893: Gender and the Colour of Art History* (1993), Griselda Pollock fait état du narratif dans l'art de Gauguin et d'autres peintres qui, comme lui, combinaient tourisme et modernisme. Au Canada comme en Europe, le voyage et le tourisme se sont accrus considérablement au tournant du siècle, dû en grande partie au prolongement des lignes de chemin de fer et à l'industrialisation accélérée des villes. De plus en plus, les citadins, dont les artistes canadiens, souhaitaient trouver refuge dans la nature. La véritable innovation canadienne a été d'incorporer dans l'art moderne un sentiment de proximité avec la nature vierge tout en bâtissant une histoire sur le concept du « lieu sauvage ».

L'un de ces lieux était le parc Algonquin ouvert en 1893 et situé à cent quarante kilomètres au nord de Toronto. En 1894, un Acte du Parlement de l'Ontario en a fait une vaste réserve forestière et faunique, un parc public susceptible de répondre à des besoins salutaires et récréatifs. Le sol et l'eau de cette immense superficie devenaient des ressources protégées, y compris les sources de cinq rivières importantes. La nature sauvage y paraissait riche de possibilités pour l'avenir – qu'il s'agisse de l'enseignement de la foresterie, de l'étude des plantes ou d'activités récréatives[26]. La création du parc a donné lieu à une véritable vénération de la nature, stimulée par des auteurs tels que l'américain James Fenimore Cooper reconnu pour ses « Leather-stocking Tales » et lu passionnément tout au long du dix-neuvième siècle. L'image de la forêt primitive de Cooper se retrouve dans les mots d'un des auteurs de l'Acte, Alexander Kirkwood. Dans une lettre de 1886 à T.B. Pardee, commissaire des Terres de la Couronne, il décrit ainsi la sombre grandeur de la forêt naturelle : « C'est en se promenant dans de tels paysages que l'esprit boit de profonds mais paisibles courants d'inspiration[27]. »

Tels ceux de l'époque victorienne, les artistes canadiens du début du vingtième siècle ont trouvé dans la nature une source constante d'images. En mai 1912, au moment même où le magazine *Saturday Night* publiait un article intitulé « A Holiday in Algonquin Park », le peintre Tom Thomson effectuait sa première visite au parc Algonquin[28]. Alors qu'il commençait à s'en inspirer, très loin de là, en Colombie-Britannique, Emily Carr s'était mise à peindre avec sympathie les objets des Premières

Nations. Déjà en 1907, à Sitka, en Alaska, elle avait résolu de recenser les mâts totémiques de la Colombie-Britannique et de 1908 à 1912, elle s'était concentrée sur ce projet extraordinairement ambitieux.

À leur façon, Thomson et Carr ont aidé à inventer notre vision du Canada et plus particulièrement d'un monde opposé à celui de la ville, un monde dans lequel dominait la vie naturelle. Des sites comme le parc Algonquin et les villages des peuples indigènes de la Colombie-Britannique, si typiquement canadien et si finement observés en peinture, offrent certaines des œuvres postimpressionnistes les plus intéressantes qui aient été peintes au Canada. Leur contemplation peut provoquer chez le spectateur des sentiments ambivalents, mais l'imagerie est devenue aujourd'hui partie intégrante du mythe canadien – un mythe comparable à une religion, qui a modelé de manière fondamentale l'organisation de notre temps libre.

Bref, le postimpressionnisme a exercé sur l'art canadien une vaste influence. Les auteurs de tableaux postimpressionnistes ont conquis un nouveau territoire, et provoqué sur la scène picturale canadienne un changement radical et d'une portée considérable. Certains plasticiens ont marqué le mouvement du sceau de leur personnalité; d'autres, poussant la circonspection presqu'à l'excès, en ont utilisé les caractéristiques sans ostentation. En réconciliant les traditions locales avec ce qui était à toutes fins pratiques un style universel, les artistes ont stimulé l'art canadien en lui injectant une vitalité nouvelle.

La directrice émérite,
The Robert McLaughlin Gallery, Oshawa,
Joan Murray

1. Voir Jacqueline V. Falkenheim, *Roger Fry and the Beginning of Formalist Art Criticism*, Ann Arbor (Michigan), 1980, cité dans Richard R. Brettell, *Modern Art 1851–1929*, Oxford, Oxford University Press, 1999, p. 21.
2. Paul Gauguin à Émile Schuffenecker, Pont-Aven, 14 août 1888, dans Françoise Cachin, *Gauguin: The Quest for Paradise*, London, Thames and Hudson, 1992, p. 176.
3. A.Y. Jackson a écrit que Cézanne, Van Gogh et d'autres modernistes étaient les dieux du Groupe des Sept. Voir Jackson à Catherine Breithaupt, Boston, 17 janvier 1921, Documents Breithaupt Bennett, Bibliothèque de l'Université de Waterloo, Waterloo, cité dans Charles C. Hill, *Le Groupe des Sept : art d'une nation*, catalogue d'exposition, Ottawa, Musée des beaux-arts du Canada, 1995, p. 24.
4. J.W. Morrice à Edmund Morris, 30 janvier 1910. Edmund Morris Letterbooks Archives, E.P. Taylor Art Reference Library, Musée des beaux-arts de l'Ontario, Toronto.
5. Voir John O'Brian, « Morrice's Pleasures (1900–1914) » dans Nicole Cloutier, et al. *James Wilson Morrice 1865-1924*, catalogue d'exposition, Montréal, Musée des beaux-arts de Montréal, 1985, p. 93.
6. Voir Louise Dompierre, *John Lyman, 1886–1967*, catalogue d'exposition, Kingston, Agnes Etherington Art Centre, 1896, p. 29.
7. Voir Xavier Girard, *Matisse: The Wonder of Colour*, New York, Gallimard, 1994, p. 58-60. Un problème se pose à propos de l'Académie Matisse. Selon Girard, le couvent qui l'abritait aurait été vendu au cours de l'été 1909, et Matisse et sa famille se seraient alors installés dans une résidence aux alentours de Paris. Or, Louise Dompierre situe au site du couvent la fréquentation de l'Académie Matisse par Lyman, très probablement durant l'hiver 1910. [Pour les dates de fréquentation de l'école par Lyman, voir Louise Dompierre, *John Lyman, 1886–1967*, catalogue d'exposition, Kingston : Agnes Etherington Art Centre, 1986, p. 31]. Lyman aurait pu être là plus tôt comme il semble être la quatrième personne à partir de la gauche

sur la photographie de Matisse et de ses étudiants à l'Académie Matisse, 1909–1910, photo Archives Matisse, Paris.

8. « Post Impressionism: Review of Movement Which Has Stirred Controversy », *Gazette*, Montréal, 30 mars 1912.

9. John Rewald, *Cézanne and America: Dealers, Collectors, Artists and Critics, 1891–1921*, Princeton : Princeton University Press, p.173.

10. « Post-Impressionists Shock Local Art Lovers at the Spring Art Exhibition », *Daily Witness*, Montréal, 26 mars 1913.

11. S. Morgan-Powell, « Art and the Post-Impressionists », *Daily Star*, Montréal, 29 mars 1913.

12. John Lyman, « To the Editor: Mr. John G. Lyman Writes in Defence of 'Post-Impressionism' », *Daily Star*, Montréal, 1er mai 1913.

13. « Pictures Will Revive Strife », *Gazette*, Montréal, 21 mai 1913.

14. S. Morgan-Powell, « Essays, Fugues, Adventures and Improvisations », *Daily Star*, Montréal, 23 mai 1913.

15. « More Post-Impressionism at the Art Gallery », *Daily Witness*, Montréal, 21 mai 1913.

16. *Daily Witness*, Montréal, 21 mai 1913.

17. S. Morgan-Powell, « A Few Notable Canvases, But a Lower Average », *Daily Star*, Montréal, 23 novembre 1913.

18. Robert Mortier, *Le Nigog* 1, 4, avril 1918, p. 119–120.

19. S. Morgan-Powell, *Daily Star*, Montréal, 23 novembre 1913.

20. Cité dans David P. Silcox, *Painting Place: The Life and Work of David B. Milne*, Toronto, University of Toronto Press, 1996, p. 387, note 23. Mon opinion diffère ici de celle de Silcox, qui voit un rapport entre la technique de composition de Milne et celle de Velazquez et Vermeer (p. 41).

21. Interview d'A.Y. Jackson par l'auteure, 4 mars 1971. Joan Murray, Documents Tom Thomson.

22. A.Y. Jackson, *A Painter's Country: The Autobiography of A.Y. Jackson*, Toronto, Vancouver, Clarke, Irwin & Company Limited, 1958, p. 47.

23. Morrice à Morris, 30 janvier 1910.

24. J'utilise le mot « environnement » au sens le plus large du terme où l'employait Marshall McLuhan, celui d'un processus actif qui est invisible. Voir Marshall McLuhan, *The Medium is the Message: An Inventory of Effects*, 1967, avec Quentin Fiore, New York, Bantam Books, 1967.

25. Peter Morrin, « An Overview: Post-Impressionism and North American Art », *The Advent of Modernism*, catalogue d'exposition, Atlanta : High Museum of Art, 1986, p.15.

26. Voir, par exemple, Thomas W. Gibson, « Algonquin National Park », *Canadian Magazine of Politics, Science, Art and Literature*, octobre 1894, p. 546.

27. A. Kirkwood, *Algonkin Forest and Park, Ontario: Letter to the Honourable T.B. Pardee, M.P.P., Commissioner of Crown Lands for Ontario*, Toronto, Warwick & Sons, 1886, p. 8.

28. « A Holiday in Algonquin Park », *Saturday Night*, 25 mai 1912, p. 4–5, 7.

Chronology

1886

Impressionism and Post-Impressionism arrive in North America simultaneously with a show loaned by the Durand-Ruel Gallery in Paris that was exhibited at the National Academy of Design in New York: Georges Seurat is represented.

1890

James Wilson Morrice arrives in Paris.

c. 1894–1895

Morrice befriends American painters Maurice Prendergast, Robert Henri and W.J. Glackens.

1903

David Milne arrives in New York where he remains until 1916.

Jugend, the German periodical, devotes the entire January issue to the Italian divisionist painter Giovanni Segantini with six paintings reproduced, four in colour and two in black and white.

Paul Gauguin dies.

c. 1903

Morrice's work changes from Impressionism to Post-Impressionism, responding to the example set by Gauguin and Henri Matisse, according to John O'Brian (see "Morrice's Pleasures," in Nicole Cloutier et al., *James Wilson Morrice, 1865–1924* [Montreal: Montreal Museum of Fine Arts, 1985], p. 93).

1904-1907

Lawren Harris studies art in Berlin. Either there or on his extensive travels through Europe, he may have seen the work of Vincent van Gogh and Paul Cézanne on exhibit, according to Peter Larisey.

1905

Critic Louis Vauxcelles applies the epithet "Les fauves" ("the wild ones") to painters in the Salon d'Automne in Paris.

1906

Roger Fry coins the term *Post-Impressionism* in an exhibition catalogue although it is more commonly associated with his show of 1910 at the Grafton Galleries, London (see 1910).

Paul Cézanne dies.

1907–1915

The Canadian Art Club, Toronto, is founded (membership in 1907 includes Franklin Brownell, Archibald Browne, James Wilson Morrice, Horatio Walker and Homer Watson).

1907

John Lyman is in Europe.

Emily Carr visits Sitka, Alaska, where for the first time she sees totem poles standing in a forested setting. They so impress her that she resolves to record all the standing totem poles in British Columbia – a project she undertakes from 1908 to 1912.

1908

The American group known as The Eight exhibit in New York.

Alfred Stieglitz opens the Little Galleries of the Photo-Secession at 291 Fifth Ave. in New York; known as 291, the gallery lasts until May 1917.

Stieglitz shows the work of Matisse (also shown in 1910 and 1911) and in 1911, watercolours by Cézanne.

1909

From May 8–18, Stieglitz shows the "Segantini-stitch" landscapes of Marsden Hartley in a one-person exhibition at Gallery 291.

John Lyman in Paris, befriends Morrice and artist Matthew Smith from Great Britain.

Probably that summer, Lyman and Matthew Smith join the Académie Matisse in Paris; Lyman remains there till January 1910.

E. Middleton Manigault has first show in New York at Haas Gallery on Madison Avenue.

1909–1910

Milne resolves to be a painter rather than a commercial illustrator.

1910

Cecil Buller attends the Art Students League, New York.

In March, Gallery 291 shows *Younger American Artists.*

In August, Emily Carr goes to Paris.

Roger Fry's exhibition *Manet and the Post-Impressionists* at the Grafton Galleries, London; the exhibition is seen by Morrice.

1911

In January, Morrice writes Edmund Morris, secretary of the Canadian Art Club, about seeing *Manet and the Post Impressionists.*

In March, the Gallery 291 shows Cézanne watercolours.

In September, A.Y. Jackson and A.H. Robinson travel to St. Malo, France.

Paris, Salon d'Automne: two Canadians represented – James Wilson Morrice and Emily Carr (*La Colline* and *Le Paysage*).

1912

Cecil Buller attends summer school of Art Students League at Woodstock, New York.

Cecil Buller and Edwin Holgate travel to Paris.

Randolph S. Hewton meets Jackson in Paris.

Emily Coonan and Mabel May study in Paris and travel to Belgium and Holland.

First discussion of Post-Impressionism in the Canadian press.

In December, Morrice makes first trip to Tangier (he returns in January and stays till February 1913; on the second trip he visits with Matisse).

1913

In January, Lawren Harris and J.E.H. MacDonald see the *Exhibition of Contemporary Scandinavian Art* at the Albright Art Gallery (now the Albright-Knox) in Buffalo.

From February 15 to March 15, the International Exhibition of Modern Art (known as the Armory Show from its place of venue) is on view in New York (touring after to Chicago and Boston); the exhibition includes Cézanne, Gauguin,

Matisse, and van Gogh, along with Canadians Ernest Lawson, E. Middleton Manigault and David Milne, among others.

From February 17 to March 1, Post-Impressionist paintings by Randolph Hewton and Jackson are shown at the Art Association of Montreal.

From March 25 to April 19, the Thirtieth Annual Spring Exhibition of the Art Association of Montreal opens (includes paintings of Randolph Hewton, A.Y. Jackson and John Lyman).

On March 26, Hewton, Jackson and Lyman and Post-Impressionism are attacked in the Montreal *Daily Witness*.

On March 29, S. Morgan-Powell scathingly criticizes Post-Impressionism in the Montreal *Daily Star* (attack continues on April 16).

From May 21 to 31, Lyman exhibits five years of work at the Art Association of Montreal.

In November, Dr. MacCallum introduces Tom Thomson to A.Y. Jackson, who is working on his painting *Terre Sauvage* in the studio of Lawren Harris at Bloor and Yonge in Toronto.

Thomson is fascinated with this important work by Jackson and returns many times to watch its progress, becoming a good friend of Jackson in the process.

Lawren Harris first uses the Segantini-stitch technique in his work.

In 1978, scholar Jeremy Adamson speculates that this technique may derive from seeing Marsden Hartley's work – which also used the Segantini-stitch – on a trip to New York to Gallery 291 (the date is unknown) or that Harris recalled Segantini's pictures in European museums (see Jeremy Adamson, *Lawren S. Harris: Urban Scenes and Wilderness Landscapes, 1906–1930* [Toronto: Art Gallery of Ontario, 1978], p. 50). Peter Larisey, however, believes that Harris would have gotten all he needed from seeing the work of van Gogh in Berlin.

1913 (?)

Middleton Manigault in Paris and Brittany.

1914

Clive Bell publishes his book, *Art*.

In January, A.Y. Jackson and Tom Thomson share Studio One at the newly opened Studio Building on Severn Street in Toronto.

War is declared on August 11.

Daniel Gallery opens in New York at No. 2 West Forty-Seventh Street (shows the work of Middleton Manigault).

Collector Ferdinand Howald, a mining engineer from Columbus, Ohio, buys his first work, a painting by Manigault.

Anne Savage begins study at the Art Association of Montreal.

1917

On July 8, Tom Thomson dies in Algonquin Park.

1918

Publication in Montreal of the avant-garde periodical *Le Nigog*, the first magazine to present art and literary criticism in French Canada (the staff includes Adrien Hébert who illustrated for the review).

1920

In March (?), the Group of Seven is founded in Toronto.

The Group of Seven's first show opens at the Art Gallery of Toronto in May (their last exhibition is in 1931).

In May, the Beaver Hall Group is founded at 305 Beaver Hall, Montreal. Their first show is in January 1921 (these quarters are rented until 1924).

Chronologie

1886

L'impressionnisme et le postimpressionnisme sont introduits simultanément en Amérique du Nord grâce à une exposition prêtée par la galerie Durand-Ruel à Paris à la National Academy of Design à New York : Georges Seurat est un des artistes représentés.

1890

James Wilson Morrice arrive à Paris.

Vers 1894–1895

Morrice se lie d'amitié avec les peintres américains Maurice Prendergast, Robert Henri et W. J. Glackens.

1903

David Milne arrive à New York, où il demeure jusqu'en 1916.

Le journal allemand *Jugend [Jeunesse]* consacre son numéro de janvier au peintre divisionniste italien Giovanni Segantini, reproduisant six tableaux du peintre, dont quatre en couleurs et deux en noir et blanc.

Paul Gauguin meurt.

Vers 1903

Morrice abandonne l'impressionnisme pour le postimpressionnisme, suivant en cela, selon John O'Brian, l'exemple de Gauguin et de Matisse (voir « Morrice's Pleasures » dans Nicole

Cloutier, *James Wilson Morrice, 1865–1924*, Montréal : Musée des beaux-arts de Montréal, 1986, p. 93).

1904–1907

Lawren Harris poursuit des études d'art à Berlin. Peter Larisey remarque qu'Harris aurait pu voir des tableaux de Vincent Van Gogh et de Paul Cézanne à Berlin ou ailleurs en Europe, alors qu'il parcourait le continent.

1905

Le critique Louis Vauxcelles utilise l'épithète « Les fauves » pour décrire les peintres exposés au Salon d'automne à Paris.

1906

Roger Fry invente le terme postimpressionnisme dans un catalogue d'exposition, bien que ce terme soit d'ordinaire associé à l'exposition que Fry organisa en 1910 aux Grafton Galleries de Londres (voir 1910).

Paul Cézanne meurt.

1907–1915

Le Canadian Art Club se constitue à Toronto (Franklin Brownell, Archibald Browne, James Wilson Morrice, Horatio Walker et Homer Watson comptent parmi ses premiers membres).

1907

John Lyman séjourne en Europe.

Emily Carr voyage à Sitka, en Alaska, où elle voit pour la première fois des mâts totémiques dans un décor forestier. Elle est tellement impressionnée qu'elle décide de cataloguer tous les mâts totémiques encore en existence en Colombie-Britannique. Ce projet va l'occuper de 1908 à 1912.

1908

Le groupe américain dit « The Eight » organise une exposition à New York.

Alfred Stieglitz inaugure ses « Little Galleries of the Photo-Secession » au 291 Fifth Avenue à New York. Il expose des tableaux de Matisse, ce qu'il fera de nouveau en 1910 et 1911. (En 1911, il présentera aussi des aquarelles de Cézanne.)

1909

Du 8 au 18 mai, il offre des paysages de Marsden Hartley réalisés selon la méthode pointilliste de Segantini (le fameux « trait de pinceau Segantini »). Appelées communément « le 291 », les Little Galleries demeureront ouvertes jusqu'en mai 1917.

John Lyman est à Paris, où il se lie d'amitié avec Morrice et l'artiste anglais Matthew Smith. Avec ce dernier, il s'inscrit à l'Académie Matisse, probablement durant l'été de l'année en cause. Lyman demeure à Paris jusqu'en janvier 1910.

E. Middleton Manigault expose pour la première fois à New York, à la Haas Gallery sur Madison Avenue.

1909–1910

Milne décide d'être peintre plutôt qu'illustrateur.

1910

Cecil Buller suit des cours à l'Art Students League à New York.

En mars, « le 291 » présente *Younger American Artists.*

En août, Emily Carr se rend à Paris.

Roger Fry présente son exposition *Manet and the Post-Impressionists* aux Grafton Galleries de Londres. Morrice visite l'exposition.

1911

En janvier, Morrice écrit à Edmund Morris, secrétaire du Canadian Art Club; il mentionne qu'il a vu l'exposition *Manet and the Post-Impressionists.*

En mars, des aquarelles de Cézanne sont présentées au « 291 ».

En septembre, A. Y. Jackson et A. H. Robinson se rendent à Saint-Malo en France.

Deux artistes canadiens – James Wilson Morrice et Emily Carr (*La Colline* et *Le Paysage*) – sont représentés au Salon d'automne de Paris.

1912

Cecil Buller suit un cours d'été à l'Art Students League à Woodstock (New York).

Cecil Buller et Edwin Holgate se rendent à Paris.

Randolph S. Hewton rencontre Jackson à Paris.

Emily Coonan et Mabel May étudient à Paris et voyagent ensuite en Belgique et dans les Pays-Bas.

La première discussion sur le postimpressionnisme apparaît dans la presse canadienne.

En décembre, Morrice effectue son premier voyage à Tanger (il y retourne de nouveau en janvier de l'année suivante et y demeure jusqu'en février 1913; lors de son second séjour, il rend visite à Matisse).

1913

En janvier, Lawren Harris et J. E. H. MacDonald visitent l'*Exhibition of Contemporary Scandinavian Art* à la Albright Art Gallery (aujourd'hui Albright-Knox) à Buffalo.

Du 15 février au 15 mars, l'*International Exhibition of Modern Art* (généralement appelée l'*Armory Show* à cause de l'endroit abritant l'exposition) est présentée à New York (puis à Chicago et à Boston). L'exposition comprend des œuvres de Cézanne, Gauguin, Matisse et Van Gogh ainsi que d'artistes canadiens dont Ernest Lawson, E. Middleton Manigault et David Milne.

Du 17 février au 1er mars, l'Art Association of Montreal présente des tableaux postimpressionnistes de Randolph Hewton et Jackson.

Du 25 mars au 19 avril, l'Art Association of Montreal tient son 30e Salon du printemps. Il offre entre autres des tableaux de Randolph Hewton, A.Y. Jackson et John Lyman.

Le 26 mars, un article dans le quotidien montréalais *Daily Witness* attaque Hewton, Jackson et le postimpressionnisme.

Le 29 mars, S. Morgan-Powell fait une critique virulente du postimpressionnisme dans le *Daily Star* de Montréal (il poursuit son attaque le 16 avril).

Du 21 au 31 mai, Lyman présente ses œuvres des quatre années précédentes à l'Art Association of Montreal.

En novembre, le Dr MacCallum présente Tom Thomson à A.Y. Jackson, alors en train de travailler à son tableau *Terre sauvage* dans l'atelier de Lawren Harris à l'angle des rues Bloor et Yonge à Toronto. Thomson est fasciné par cette toile importante et revient souvent voir Jackson pour en observer le développement. Ils deviennent de bons amis.

Lawren Harris commence à utiliser la technique du « trait de

pinceau Segantini ». [En 1978, l'expert Jeremy Adamson suggère qu'Harris aurait pu prendre connaissance de cette technique lors d'une visite à la galerie « 291 » de New York (date inconnue). Il aurait vu alors les tableaux de Marsden Hartley qui font une utilisation évidente du « trait de pinceau Segantini ». Une autre possibilité selon Adamson serait qu'Harris se serait rappelé les œuvres de Segantini aperçues dans des musées européens (voir Jeremy Adamson, *Lawren S. Harris: Urban Scenes and Wilderness Landscapes, 1906–1930* (Toronto: Musée des beaux-arts de l'Ontario, 1978), p. 50]. Par contre, Peter Larisey est convaincu qu'Harris aurait appris tout ce qu'il lui fallait de l'œuvre de Van Gogh vue durant son séjour à Berlin.

1913 (?)

Middleton Manigault se trouve à Paris et en Bretagne.

1914

Clive Bell publie son livre *Art*.

En janvier, A.Y. Jackson et Tom Thomson partagent le « Studio One » dans le nouvel immeuble d'ateliers de la rue Severn à Toronto.

La Première Guerre mondiale est déclarée le 11 août.

La Daniel Gallery est inaugurée à New York, au 2 West Forty-Seventh Street (présentation de tableaux de Middleton Manigault). Le collectionneur Ferdinand Howald, un ingénieur des mines de Columbus (Ohio), achète sa première œuvre, un tableau de Manigault.

Anne Savage commence ses études à l'Art Association of Montreal.

1917

Le 8 juillet, Tom Thomson décède dans le parc Algonquin.

1918

La revue d'avant-garde *Le Nigog* est lancée à Montréal. Il s'agit du premier magazine de critique artistique et littéraire au Canada français. (Membre de l'équipe de rédaction, Adrien Hébert fournit régulièrement des dessins).

1920

Le Groupe des Sept naît à Toronto en mars (?). La première exposition a lieu au Musée des beaux-arts de Toronto en mai (la dernière exposition a lieu en 1931).

En mai, le Groupe de Beaver Hall voit le jour au 305 Beaver Hall à Montréal, endroit qu'il louera jusqu'en 1924. Le groupe tiendra sa première exposition en janvier 1921.

The Artists at the Birth of the Modern

Les artistes associés à la naissance de la modernité

Cecil Buller
Franklin Carmichael
Emily Carr
Emily Coonan
Lawren Harris
Adrien Hébert
Randolph S. Hewton
Edwin H. Holgate
A.Y. Jackson
Arthur Lismer
John Lyman
J.E.H. MacDonald
F.H. McGillivray
E. Middleton Manigault
H. Mabel May
David Milne
James Wilson Morrice
A.H. Robinson
Anne Savage
Tom Thomson

Cecil Buller

1920s / LES ANNÉES 1920

Both as a printmaker and a painter, Cecil Buller (1886–1973) showed herself to be an intelligent student of wider trends. Born in Montreal, she seems to have first studied art in Paris in 1902. She was a student of the progressive teacher William Brymner, the director of the Art Association of Montreal from 1886 to 1921, and was probably introduced to Post-Impressionism by him. His belief that his training should prepare the student for study abroad and his encouragement doubtless led to Buller's enrollment at the Art Students League in New York in 1910, and at the League's Summer School at Woodstock in 1912. From an early age, too, she was involved with artistic circles in Montreal and she counted Edwin Holgate and Randolph Hewton among her friends: both of them were artists with whom she would have discussed the new art. In 1912, on a trip to Paris in the company of Holgate, she learned first-hand about the Post-Impressionists and Cubists. In 1915, she applied her knowledge of Post-Impressionism to her own painting, using broad areas of paint, a flat decorative effect, and strong colour. *Market, Concarneau,* which likely dates from that year, was painted in Brittany, a favourite haunt of artists. It recalls the work of Maurice Denis, a member of the Nabis group who admired Gauguin and Cézanne, and with whom Buller studied.[1] The painting, according to Charles C. Hill, shows a clear understanding of the work of Denis and recalls the work of Emile Bernard.[2] Commenting on her depiction of carts encircling the interwoven arrangement of Breton women, Hill notes that both form and space are radically flattened and colour is simplified.

Buller's earliest known print also dates from 1915. In that year, she turned full-time to printmaking. In 1918, she settled in New York. Her wood engravings in the early 1920s of nudes in the landscape show her sympathy with the aims of Gauguin, as expressed, for example, in the woodcut series he carved for *Noa Noa* in the early 1890s. She also combined the nude figure with machine-age imagery. In 1959, Buller resettled in Montreal.

1. On her National Gallery of Canada biography form in 1920, Cecil Buller states that her studies included a period of work with Maurice Denis in Paris. See Patricia Ainslie, *Cecil Buller: Modernist Printmaker* (Calgary: Glenbow Museum, 1989), p. 10; for a discussion of what Buller saw in Paris in 1912, see p. 14. Ainslie suggests that Buller remained in Paris until 1916. She suggests that through Denis, Buller was influenced by Gauguin's method of using flat areas of colour with figures defined by line (p. 16). She also notes in Buller's prints the influence of Cézanne.

2. Cecil Buller Accession file, Curatorial files, National Gallery of Canada, Ottawa. Hill notes that Denis taught at the Académie Ranson from 1909 to 1919. Possibly Buller studied privately with Denis since she does not mention the school.

1. *Market, Concarneau*, c. 1915 / *Marché à Concarneau*, v. 1915

Cecil Buller

En gravure comme en peinture, Cecil Buller (1886–1973) donne l'impression d'une artiste intellligente, avide d'explorer de nouveaux horizons. Née à Montréal, elle semble avoir étudié les beaux-arts à Paris dès 1902. Il est probable qu'elle a d'abord entendu parler du postimpressionnisme dans la classe de William Brymner, professeur aux idées avancées qui de 1886 à 1921 a dirigé l'Art Association of Montreal. Il croyait que la formation qu'il donnait à ses étudiants devait les préparer à étudier à l'étranger, et ses encouragements ont dû pousser Buller à s'inscrire à l'Art Students League de New York en 1910, puis aux cours d'été de la League à Woodstock en 1912. Dès ses débuts, Buller a fréquenté les cercles artistiques montréalais où elle comptait parmi ses amis Edwin Holgate et Randolph Newton avec qui elle aurait sans doute examiné le nouveau mouvement d'art. En 1912, à la faveur d'un voyage à Paris en compagnie d'Holgate, elle a pris directement connaissance du travail des postimpressionnistes et des cubistes. En 1915, elle a appliqué les principes du postimpressionnisme dans ses propres tableaux, peignant de vastes surfaces en y combinant des effets décoratifs et de fortes couleurs. Réalisé en Bretagne, l'un des endroits de prédilection des peintres, *Marché à Concarneau* date vraisemblablement de cette année-là. Il rappelle l'œuvre de Maurice Denis, membre du groupe Nabis qui admirait Gauguin et Cézanne et auprès duquel a étudié[1] Buller. Selon Charles C. Hill, le tableau dénote une nette compréhension de l'œuvre de Denis tout en évoquant celle d'Émile Bernard[2]. Il remarque que la forme et l'espace sont tout à fait plats et que la couleur y est simplifiée : les charrettes encerclent les silhouettes entremêlées des bretonnes.

La première gravure qu'on connaisse de Buller date de 1915, année à partir de laquelle l'artiste s'est consacrée à plein temps à cette forme d'art. En 1918, elle s'est installée à New York. Ses gravures sur bois du début des années vingt, qui représentent des nus dans un paysage, font état de son affinité avec les buts que poursuivait Gauguin, tels qu'exemplifiés dans la série qu'il a gravée pour *Noa Noa* au début des années 1890. Buller a aussi combiné le nu avec l'imagerie d'un monde mécanisé. Elle est revenue s'installer à Montréal en 1959.

1. Dans le formulaire biographique de 1920 de la Galerie nationale du Canada, Cecil Buller indique, dans la description de ses études, qu'elle a travaillé avec Maurice Denis à Paris. Voir Patricia Ainslie, *Cecil Buller: Modernist Printmaker* (catalogue d'exposition) (Calgary : Glenbow Museum, 1989), p. 10. Pour une discussion de ce que Buller a vu à Paris en 1912, voir Ainslie (p. 14). De l'avis d'Ainslie, Buller serait demeurée à Paris jusqu'en 1916 et aurait appris de Denis que Gauguin employait des zones colorées bidimensionnelles où la ligne servait à définir les personnages, idée qu'elle a incorporée dans ses propres œuvres (p. 16). Ainslie note aussi l'influence de Cézanne dans les gravures de Buller.

2. Cecil Buller, Dossier du conservateur, Musée des beaux-arts du Canada, Ottawa. Hill remarque que Denis a enseigné à l'Académie Ranson de 1909 à 1919. Comme Buller ne mentionne pas l'école, il est possible qu'elle ait plutôt suivi des cours privés avec Denis.

Franklin Carmichael

Antwerp, c. 1915 / Anvers, v. 1915

Group of Seven member Franklin Carmichael (1890–1945) was first known in art circles as a friend of Tom Thomson, with whom he worked at Grip Ltd. and shared a studio (in 1915). From Thomson and other members of the nascent Group of Seven who worked at Grip, artists such as J.E.H. MacDonald and Arthur Lismer, he would likely have learned of the new developments in art. Megan Bice in *Light & Shadow: The Work of Franklin Carmichael*, her catalogue for the 1990 retrospective at the McMichael Canadian Art Collection, suggests that in Carmichael's 1915 oil panel *Bittersweet Berries* (Private Collection), in which the two-dimensional patterning of the branch of berries is combined with sensitive contours, the artist echoed the contrasts found in both Japanese art and the Post-Impressionist aesthetic. Contact with Thomson would have influenced Carmichael in his handling of colour (in *Bittersweet Berries*, the colour is boldly handled and of a reduced range) and way of structuring the landscape. Carmichael also absorbed one of Thomson's favourite compositional motifs – the distant view seen through a foreground screen of foliage – and used it effectively in works like *Sumachs* (McMichael Canadian Art Collection) and *Winter Hillside*. In 1920, in paintings like *Autumn Sunlight* (Private Collection), he began to assert his own personality, combining Thomson's fiery colour effects with more geometrically shaped clouds. It was in *Autumn Hillside* of 1920 (Art Gallery of Ontario) that Carmichael achieved his first use of the pictorial motif that he was to use often in his later work: a bank of cloud (here, lavender in colour) that lifts like a curtain to reveal clear sky and rolling hills. The rhetoric is high Canadian style. The untitled sketch, which is related to works Carmichael painted in the early 1920s, shows first-hand the way in which he combined colour and strongly simplified form. In *The Glade*, he aimed at an expansive embrace of Canadian light and colour in a view of a wooded interior: the effect is of a decorative and a strongly patterned rendering of immediate facts.

2. *Winter Hillside*, 1918 (?) / *Colline en hiver*, 1918 (?)

3. *Untitled*, c. 1920 / *Sans titre*, v. 1920

4. *The Glade*, c. 1922 / *La Clairière*, v. 1922

Franklin Carmichael

Membre du Groupe des Sept, Franklin Carmichael (1890–1945) s'est d'abord fait connaître dans les cercles artistiques grâce à son amitié avec Tom Thomson, avec qui il a travaillé chez Grip Ltd. et partagé un atelier en 1915. C'est vraisemblement par Thomson et les autres membres du nouveau Groupe des Sept qui travaillaient chez Grip, tels que J.E.H. MacDonald et Arthur Lismer, qu'il aurait été mis au fait des récents courants artistiques. Selon Megan Bice, l'huile sur panneau du peintre intitulée *Bittersweet Berries* (*Baies aigres-douces*, 1915, collection privée) évoquerait les contrastes que l'on trouve dans l'art japonais comme dans l'esthétique postimpressionniste – le patron bidimensionnel de la branche de baies s'allie à des contours délicats. En partageant un atelier avec Thomson, Carmichael aurait subi l'influence de ce dernier dans son utilisation de la couleur (dans *Baies aigres-douces*, la couleur, d'une palette modérée, est appliquée avec audace) et sa façon de structurer le paysage. Carmichael a aussi incorporé l'un des motifs de composition favoris de Thomson – à savoir, une vue lointaine aperçue à travers un écran de feuillage à l'avant-plan – et l'a employé efficacement dans des peintures comme *Sumachs* (Collection McMichael d'art canadien) et *Colline en hiver*. En 1920, dans des tableaux tels que *Soleil d'automne* (collection privée), Carmichael a commencé de s'affirmer, en combinant les effets de couleurs violentes de Thomson avec des nuages de forme géométrique plus accusée. C'est dans *Colline en automne* en 1920 (Musée des beaux-arts de l'Ontario) qu'il a utilisé pour la première fois le motif pictural qui allait plus tard caractériser son œuvre : un banc de nuages (ici de couleur lavende) se levant tel un rideau pour révéler un ciel clair et des collines ondulées. C'est le style canadien par excellence. L'esquisse sans titre fait partie des œuvres de Carmichael réalisées au début des années vingt; elle démontre clairement la manière du peintre de travailler la couleur et une forme largement simplifiée. Dans *La Clairière*, l'artiste vise à créer une image exubérante de la lumière et des couleurs typiquement canadiennes se dégageant d'un intérieur boisé : le résultat est décoratif tout en représentant une situation réelle rendue au moyen de formes fortes.

Emily Carr

1930

By 1911 Emily Carr (1871–1945), who lived in Victoria on Vancouver Island, was already an *aficionado* of Post-Impressionist style as indicated by her high-keyed palette. This development in Carr's work followed periods of study in California and England. She arrived in Paris in 1910, armed with a letter to the British painter Henry Phelan Gibb, contact with whom brought her into the artistic milieu of Post-Impressionism and Fauvism. Her first month was spent as a student at the Académie Colarossi. She then joined the private studio of the Scottish artist John Duncan Fergusson. He had begun teaching with the portrait painter Jacques-Emile Blanche at La Palette and invited Carr to join him there as a student. But Carr found her real inspiration in 1911 working in Crécy-en-Brie, a little village outside Paris, painting landscapes with Gibb. That year she travelled to Brittany in the company of Gibb and his wife and studied under New Zealand expatriate Frances Hodgkins at Concarneau. The trip enriched her work: in combination with a looser finish, the colour in her paintings became more dynamic and playful. This approach to colour and handling is particularly evident in *Brittany, Kitchen* (Private Collection), for instance, where Carr has applied yellow-gold and orange to represent the surface of the walls, yellow to the sunlit sections and purple to the shadows.

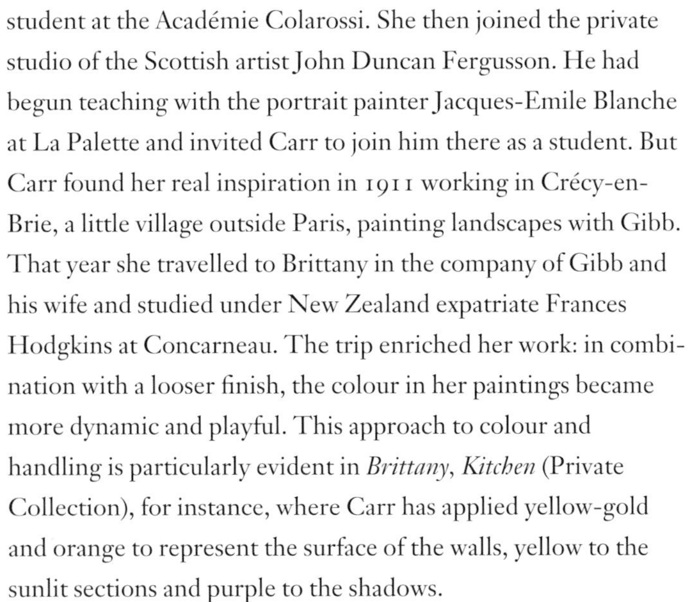

With Morrice, Carr showed her work at the 1911 Salon d'Automne in Paris along with artists such as Maurice Vlaminck. Vigorous in colour – with dramatic purples, oranges, and greens or reds, and dark blues – and with flat planes and strong contours, her paintings now reflected her new absorption of Post-Impressionism. The change in style opened her work up to "brighter, cleaner colour, simpler form [and] more intensity," as she wrote in her book *Growing Pains*.[1] During this moment, she was intimately in touch with the artistic vanguard. Upon her return to Canada in 1912, she came back to an idea that was inspired by a visit in 1899 to Ucluelet on the West Coast of Vancouver Island and that was reinforced by a cruise she made to Alaska in 1907. She began to paint the totem poles that stood in the villages of the First Nations peoples of British Columbia, attempting to document as many as she could. Her project to create a historic record of the poles was also a romantic quest to understand the First Nations inhabitants of the region. She turned her attention as well to the landscape of the West Coast in paintings such as *Trees*, conveying its singular qualities, always with vigorous brushwork, vibrant colour and strong design.

Carr's totem pole paintings embody the ambiguous relationship in her work between modernism and the culture of the First Nations. She eliminated any reference to First Nations contact with the modern world, presenting instead an idealized picture

of an idyllic existence. Even while she was creating her paeans to a disappearing world, Canada, through its policies of assimilation and rejection of the potlatch and other indigenous practices, was deliberately suppressing the culture of the First Nations. Recently, Jay Stewart and Peter Macnair curated an exhibition for the Art Gallery of Greater Victoria titled *To the Totem Forests: Emily Carr and Contemporaries Interpret Coastal Villages* in which they drew attention to the accuracy of Carr's depiction.

The brilliantly coloured *Yan, Q.C.I.*, with its totem pole placed prominently in the centre of the composition, may have derived from a field sketch recorded during a trip to the Queen Charlottes. The sketch was later transformed in the studio into this major work, a painting that captures the essence of Northwest monumental sculpture.

1. Emily Carr, *Growing Pains* (Toronto: Oxford, 1946), p. 306.

5. *Breton Farm Yard*, 1912 (?) / *Cour de ferme bretonne*, 1912 (?)

6. *Yan, Q.C.I*, 1912

7. *Trees*, 1919 / *Arbres*, 1919

Emily Carr

Déjà en 1911, Emily Carr (1871–1945), originaire de Victoria sur l'Île de Vancouver, affectionnait le postimpressionnisme, comme en témoigne sa palette aux couleurs fortes. Ce goût pour le nouveau langage pictural s'est manifesté chez elle à la suite de stages d'études en Californie et en Angleterre. En 1910, elle est arrivée à Paris munie d'une lettre du peintre britannique Henry Phelan Gibb, dont la réputation a facilité son entrée dans le milieu artistique du postimpressionnisme et du fauvisme. Le premier mois de son séjour, elle a étudié à l'Académie Colarossi. Elle a ensuite fréquenté l'atelier privé de l'artiste écossais John Duncan Fergusson, qui l'invita à le suivre à la Palette où il avait commencé à enseigner avec le portraitiste Jacques-Émile Blanche. Mais c'est en 1911 que Carr s'est vraiment découverte, en peignant des paysages avec Gibb à Crécy-en-Brie, un petit village à l'extérieur de Paris. Cette même année, elle a accompagné Gibb et son épouse en Bretagne, et étudié à Concarneau avec Frances Hodgkins, expatriée de la Nouvelle-Zélande. Ce voyage a enrichi et libéré sa couleur, qui s'est faite plus dynamique, plus enjouée, et moins léchée. Ainsi, dans *Bretagne, cuisine* (collection privée), Carr a utilisé le jaune or et l'orange pour représenter les surfaces murales, le jaune pour rendre les sections ensoleillées et le violet pour suggérer les ombres.

Tel Morrice, et la même année que lui, en 1911, Carr a exposé à Paris au Salon d'Automne, aux côtés d'artistes comme Maurice Vlaminck. Ses motifs, rendus au moyen de zones plates, de contours affirmés et de couleurs vigoureuses et dramatiques dont des violets, des oranges, des verts ou des rouges et des bleus foncés, dénotent son assimilation des techniques postimpressionnistes. Comme Carr l'a noté dans son livre *Growing Pains*[1], ce changement de style a donné lieu chez elle « à des couleurs plus pures et plus éclatantes, à une forme plus simple, et à une intensité plus grande ». Elle était alors en contact avec l'avant-garde artistique. À son retour au Canada en 1912, elle est revenue à une idée qu'elle avait conçue en 1899 lors d'une visite à Ucluelet sur la côte ouest de l'Île de Vancouver et qu'avait renforcée une croisière en Alaska en 1907. Elle s'est mise à peindre, dans les villages des Premières Nations en Colombie-Britannique, le plus grand nombre de mâts totémiques préservés que possible. Son projet de faire des mâts un document historique tenait d'un désir romantique de compréhension des Premières Nations. Comme le démontre le tableau *Arbres*, elle s'est aussi intéressée au paysage de la côte ouest dont elle a chaque fois rendu les qualités particulières au moyen de coups de pinceau vigoureux, de couleurs vives et d'un dessin affirmé.

Les mâts totémiques de Carr expriment les rapports ambigus du modernisme et de la culture indigène. L'artiste a éliminé de sa peinture tout contact des Premières Nations avec le monde moderne au profit d'une représentation idyllique et mythique de leur existence. Elle a créé ces tableaux au moment même où le Canada, par ses politiques d'assimilation et de rejet des potlatch et autres pratiques de la culture indigène, tâchait de supprimer la culture des Premières Nations. Récemment les conservateurs Jay Stewart et Peter Macnair ont discuté la justesse des renditions de Carr à la faveur de l'exposition *To the Totem Forests: Emily Carr and Contemporaries Interpret Coastal Villages*, qu'ils ont présentée à l'Art Gallery of Greater Victoria. Il se peut que Carr soit allée aux Îles de la Reine-Charlotte et qu'elle ait réalisé sur

place un croquis qu'elle aurait ensuite repris en studio pour *Yan, Q.C.I* (Îles de la Reine-Charlotte). Cet important tableau, dans lequel elle a placé le mât à l'avant-plan du tableau et utilisé de brillantes couleurs, saisit l'essence de la sculpture monumentale du Nord-Ouest.

1. Emily Carr, *Growing Pains* (Toronto : Oxford, 1946), p. 306.

Emily Coonan

Emily Coonan (1885–1917) had been introduced to Post-Impressionism by 1912, a relatively early date for artists in Canada. She was one of the star pupils of William Brymner at the Art Association of Montreal, and a member of the Beaver Hall Group founded in 1920. From August 1912 to about Christmas time of that year, and along with Mabel May, she had worked in Paris. Karen Antaki suggests that they then travelled to Northern France, Belgium and Holland.[1] Two paintings, *Girl with a Rose* and *Girl in Green*, which Coonan painted in 1913 and showed at the Royal Canadian Academy exhibition of that year, suggest that the trip gave new direction to her work, although Coonan's use of Post-Impressionism is generalized in its effect. *Girl with a Rose*, in which she boldly summarized in paint the fabric of the dress and the sitter's right hand, gives the gist of Coonan's style. As Antaki has pointed out, she looked to the formal investigations of the European moderns, which she expressed in an intimate, meditative tone, capturing a muted but expressive mood. David Rozniatowski appropriately describes Coonan's work as imparting a sullen Brontë-esque quality to her subjects.[2] Coonan's work is skilfully handled with painterly nuance; her colours carefully orchestrated. In 1914, Coonan received the travelling scholarship given by the trustees of the National Gallery of Canada. Doubtless, if she had been able to take up the award, she would have continued her study of Post-Impressionism abroad. The First World War broke out, however, and she was not able to use the prize till 1920.

1. Karen Antaki, "Rediscovering Emily Coonan," *Emily Coonan (1885–1971)* (Montreal: Concordia Art Gallery, Concordia University, 1987), p. 22.
2. David Rozniatowski, "Art History Lite," *BorderCrossings* 19, 3 (August 2000), p. 83.

8. *Girl with a Rose*, 1913 / *Jeune fille à la rose*, 1913

9. *Girl in Green*, c. 1913 / *Jeune fille en vert*, v. 1913

Emily Coonan

Emily Coonan (1885–1917) a subi l'influence du postimpressionnisme en 1912, plus tôt que plusieurs autres artistes canadiens. Elle comptait parmi les meilleurs élèves de William Brymner à l'Art Association of Montreal, et fut membre du Groupe de Beaver Hall fondé en 1920. En 1912, du mois d'août jusqu'aux environs de Noël, elle a travaillé à Paris avec Mabel May. Karen Antaki croit qu'elles auraient ensuite voyagé ensemble dans le nord de la France, ainsi qu'en Belgique et dans les Pays-Bas[1]. Deux tableaux, *Jeune fille à la rose* et *Jeune fille en vert*, peints en 1913 et présentés la même année à l'exposition de l'Académie royale des arts du Canada, laissent croire que la peinture de Coonan a pris une nouvelle direction à la suite du voyage, bien que son utilisation des techniques postimpressionnistes ne soit pas vraiment spécifique. Dans *Jeune fille à la rose*, son application de la peinture traduit avec force le tissu de la robe et la main droite du modèle, et le tableau livre l'essentiel de Coonan. Comme le remarque Antaki, l'artiste a rendu les recherches formelles des modernistes européens d'une manière intime et méditative, créant une atmosphère sourde mais expressive. David Rozniatowski décrit à juste titre les personnages de Coonan comme ayant l'air maussade de certains personnages de Brontë[2]. L'œuvre de Coonan se caractérise par ses nuances picturales et ses couleurs soigneusement orchestrées. En 1914, l'artiste a reçu une bourse de voyage du conseil d'administration de la Galerie nationale du Canada. Nul doute que si elle avait pu tout de suite en profiter, elle aurait poursuivi ses études du postimpressionnisme à l'étranger, mais la Première Guerre mondiale a fait en sorte qu'elle n'a pu utiliser son prix avant 1920.

1. Karen Antaki, « Rediscovering Emily Coonan », *Emily Coonan (1885–1971)* (catalogue d'exposition) (Montréal : Galerie d'art Concordia, Université Concordia, 1987), p. 22.

2. David Rozniatowski, « Art History Lite », *BorderCrossings* 19, 3 (août 2000), p. 83.

Lawren (Stewart) Harris

Studio Building, Toronto, c. 1920/
immeuble de studios, Toronto, vers 1920

Lawren Harris (1885–1970) trained in Berlin from 1904 to 1907. While there he would have had access to exhibitions of the great moderns, among them Gauguin, van Gogh, Cézanne, and other European Post-Impressionists. Peter Larisey suggests he would also have been exposed to modern German art during this period.[1] His brush stroke may have been influenced by van Gogh, though this would have emerged in his work much later – likely in 1913. Another point of view is taken by Jeremy Adamson who believes that Harris was strongly influenced by the "stitch" technique of the Italian Post-Impressionist Giovanni Segantini (1858–1899).[2] Segantini used a thick "stitch" brush stroke of parallel lines of colour and juxtaposed complementary hues that he combined with a naturalistic style suffused with mystical overtones. Harris, who studied in Berlin in 1904, might have seen Segantini's paintings reproduced in the German periodical *Jugend* which gave Segantini's work a full issue in January 1903 and reproduced his work in the period 1906–1907.[3] Harris may also have learned of Segantini more directly, perhaps on a visit to New York during which he saw Alfred Stieglitz's Little Galleries of the Photo-Secession (known as 291 from its address at 291 Fifth Avenue). If the trip took place between 1912 and 1914, he could have seen on exhibit in 291 the work of Marsden Hartley, which showed the influence of Segantini. Harris's vigorous use of paint and bold strokes seem more akin to Hartley's Segantini-influenced work than to the work of Segantini himself. On the other hand, the sympathy Harris shows in his painting to what we may think of as the influence of Post-Impressionism or Segantini may come from his experience of Scandinavian art: we know that Harris visited the *Exhibition of Contemporary Scandinavian Art* at the Albright Art Gallery in Buffalo in 1913 in the company of J.E.H. MacDonald. Both artists found the show compelling. Because of this exhibition, Harris began to proselytize for the development of a national school in painting that found as its primary subject, the landscape.

By 1917, writes Brian Foss, Harris's attention extended to the North American art movement known as "Synchromism."[4] Harris read a catalogue essay by Willard Huntington Wright who championed pathfinders among the Post-Impressionists, especially Cézanne. Adamson suggests that in 1917, Harris painted several landscapes that reveal his continued reliance on principles of decorative design, such as *Kempenfelt Bay*, c. 1917.[5] *Autumn [Kempenfelt Bay, Lake Simcoe]*, c. 1916–1917, would fit

this group. By the time of his Algoma landscapes (1918–1922), he had consolidated what would become his distinctive contribution to the Group of Seven, formed in 1920. He was often to favour the use of a rich range of tints to record the brilliant effects of light, which he combined with a strong structural sense. In *Hubert, Above Montreal Falls*, for instance, he captures the fugitive effects of bright daylight on the gorgeous colours of autumn leaves, rapidly flowing water and racing clouds. The intense contrasts contribute to an exciting effect.

In 1933, Harris helped found the Canadian Group of Painters. From 1934 to 1938, he lived in Hanover, New Hampshire, where in 1936 he turned to abstraction. In 1938, he moved to Santa Fe, New Mexico, where he joined the Transcendental Painting Group. In 1940 he settled permanently in Vancouver.

1. Conversation with Peter Larisey, Toronto, 1999.

2. Jeremy Adamson, *Lawren S. Harris: Urban Scenes and Wilderness Landscapes 1906–1930* (Toronto: Art Gallery of Ontario, 1978), p. 50.

3. Conversation with Charles C. Hill, National Gallery of Canada, Ottawa, 15 October 1999. Hill notes that Harris may have seen the periodical at the Arts and Letters Club in Toronto, to which he belonged – the Club had a subscription to the magazine – or seen the magazine through friends like MacDonald or Carmichael who owned copies.

4. Brian Foss, "'Synchromism' in Canada: Lawren Harris, Decorative Landscape, and Willard Huntington Wright, 1916–1917," *Journal of Canadian Art History* 20, 1 & 2 (1999), pp. 68–88.

5. Adamson, *Lawren S. Harris*, p. 72.

10. *Autumn [Kempenfelt Bay, Lake Simcoe]*, c. 1916–1917 / *Automne [Baie Kempenfelt, Lac Simcoe]*, v. 1916–1917

11. *Snow*, 1917 (?) / *La Neige*, 1917 (?)

12. *Hubert, Above Montreal Falls*, c. 1919 / *Hubert, Au-dessus des chutes de Montréal*, v. 1919

Lawren (Stewart) Harris

De 1904 à 1907, Lawren Harris (1885–1970) a étudié à Berlin où, selon Peter Larisey[1], il a pu voir les expositions des grands modernistes dont Gauguin, Van Gogh, Cézanne et d'autres postimpressionnistes européens, ainsi que des œuvres allemandes contemporaines. Son coup de pinceau a pu être influencé par Van Gogh, mais plus tard seulement – en 1913. Par contre, Jeremy Adamson croit qu'Harris aurait plutôt été fortement influencé par la technique du divisionnisme de l'italien postimpressionniste Giovanni Segantini (1858–1899)[2]. La peinture de Segantini se caractérise par des lignes de couleur parallèles appliquées avec un épais pinceau « divisionniste », des tons complémentaires juxtaposés et un style naturaliste imprégné de mysticisme. Il est possible qu'Harris, qui étudiait à Berlin en 1904, ait vu les tableaux de Segantini dans la revue allemande *Jugend (Jeunesse)*, qui avait consacré à Segantini son numéro de janvier 1903 et reproduit ensuite son œuvre en 1906 et 1907[3]. Harris pourrait encore s'être familiarisé avec l'œuvre de Segantini lors d'une visite aux Little Galleries of the Photo-Secession d'Alfred Stieglitz à New York (endroit communément appelé le « 291 » à cause de son adresse au 291 Fifth Avenue). À supposer que ce voyage ait eu lieu entre 1912 et 1914, Harris aurait pu voir l'exposition de Marsden Hartley, dont la peinture reflète l'influence de Segantini. En fait, la manière vigoureuse qu'a Harris d'appliquer la peinture à grands coups de brosse se rapproche davantage de l'utilisation qu'Hartley fait de Segantini que de Segantini lui-même. Par ailleurs, les affinités que les tableaux d'Harris paraissent démontrer avec Segantini ou le postimpressionnisme dénoteraient peut-être plutôt une influence de l'art scandinave : on sait qu'en 1913 Harris a visité avec J.E.H. MacDonald l'*Exhibition of contemporary Scandinavian Art* à l'Albright Art Gallery de Buffalo, et que tous deux en sont sortis fascinés. C'est d'ailleurs à la suite de cette exposition qu'Harris s'est mis à œuvrer en faveur de l'établissement d'une école nationale de peinture centrée sur le paysage.

Brian Foss écrit qu'en 1917 Harris s'intéressait aussi au mouvement nord-américain connu sous le nom de « synchronisme »[4], et qu'il avait lu dans un catalogue un essai de Willard Huntington Wright qui se faisait le champion des pionniers postimpressionnistes, plus particulièrement de Cézanne. Adamson suggère qu'en 1917 Harris a peint plusieurs paysages qui, tel *Baie Kempenfelt*, vers 1917[5], témoignent de sa fidélité aux principes du dessin décoratif. *Automne* [*Baie Kempenfelt, Lac Simcoe*], vers 1916–1917 appartiendrait à ce groupe. Lors de l'époque des paysages d'Algoma (1918–1922), Harris avait consolidé sa contribution particulière au Groupe des Sept, formé en 1920. Il devait souvent privilégier l'emploi d'une riche gamme de teintes pour rendre les brillants effets de la lumière, emploi qu'il a combiné avec un sens structural puissant. Dans *Hubert, Au-dessus des chutes de Montréal*, par exemple, il saisit les effets fuyants de la lumière du jour sur les feuilles d'automne aux couleurs somptueuses, l'eau au cours rapide et les nuages en mouvement à travers le ciel. L'intensité des contrastes contribue au saisissant résultat.

En 1933, Harris a aidé à fonder le Groupe des Peintres canadiens. De 1934 à 1938, il a vécu à Hanover, dans le New Hampshire, et en 1936 il s'est tourné vers l'abstrait comme moyen d'expression. En 1938, il a déménagé à Santa Fe, au Nouveau-

Mexique, où il s'est joint au Transcendental Painting Group. En 1940, il s'est installé pour de bon à Vancouver.

1. Conversation avec Peter Larisey, Toronto, 1999.

2. Jeremy Adamson, *Lawren S. Harris: Urban Scenes and Wilderness Landscapes 1906–1930* (catalogue d'exposition) (Toronto : Musée des beaux-arts de l'Ontario, 1978), p. 50.

3. Conversation avec Charles C. Hill, Musée des beaux-arts du Canada, Ottawa, 15 octobre 1999. Hill note qu'Harris aurait pu voir cette revue à un club dont il était membre – l'Arts and Letters Club de Toronto qui était abonné à *Jugend* – ou qu'il l'aurait pu l'apercevoir chez des amis comme MacDonald ou Carmichael qui en possédaient des exemplaires.

4. Brian Foss, « 'Synchronism' in Canada: Lawren Harris, Decorative Landscape and Willard Huntington Wright, 1916–1917 », *Journal of Canadian Art History* 20, 1 & 2 (1999), p. 68–88.

5. Adamson, *Lawren S. Harris*, p. 72.

Adrien Hébert

Early 1920s / Au début des années 1920

Born in Paris, Adrien Hébert (1890–1967) was the son of Louis-Philippe Hébert and brother of Henri Hébert, both of whom were sculptors. Hébert was a student of William Brymner at the Art Association of Montreal from 1907 to 1911. In 1911, he left Montreal for study in France (1912–1914). In Paris, he attended the École des Beaux-Arts, in the classes of Fernand Cormon, a painter of historical subjects, among others. In 1914, he returned to Montreal and taught drawing at the Conseil des arts and manufactures, and in 1917 (and until 1954) he was appointed to the position of drawing teacher by the Montreal Academic Committee and taught at the Montreal Catholic School Commission.

Hébert's interest in Post-Impressionism dates from his trip to Paris, according to Jean-René Ostiguy.[1] While a student at the École des Beaux-Arts, he became an admirer of Puvis de Chavannes and younger artists like Maurice Denis and Xavier Roussel. Ostiguy believes that Hébert would have seen the great curtain Roussel created for the Comédie des Champs-Élysées, which opened in 1913. He would also have seen the work of Edouard Vuillard at the Comédie des Champs-Élysées. However, the first manifestations of Post-Impressionism in Hébert's work, showing primarily the influence of Cézanne, occur later – in 1917, in his landscapes of Percé.[2] As an illustrator for the avant-garde Montreal review *Le Nigog*, Hébert would have been well aware of the warm interest manifested by his friend French painter Robert Mortier in Cézanne's work (Mortier wrote an article in the magazine praising Cézanne for his tenacity). Hébert's *L'Enclos, Île Bélair* reveals his knowledge of Cézanne's structural innovations. The "Enclos" was his parents' cottage on Belair Island in the Thousand Islands.

1. Jean-René Ostiguy, *Modernism in Quebec Art, 1916 to 1946* (Ottawa: National Gallery of Canada, 1982), p. 32.
2. Jean-René Ostiguy, *Adrien Hébert: Thirty Years of His Art, 1923–1953* (Ottawa: National Gallery of Canada, 1971), p. 11.

13. *"Enclos," Belair Island, 1921* / *L'Enclos, Île Bélair*, 1921

Adrien Hébert

Né à Paris, Adrien Hébert (1890–1967), fils de Louis-Philippe Hébert et frère d'Henri Hébert, l'un et l'autre sculpteurs, a d'abord étudié de 1907 à 1911 avec William Brymner à l'Art Association of Montreal, puis de 1912 à 1914 à l'École des Beaux-Arts de Paris où il a suivi les classes de Fernand Cormon, peintre de sujets historiques. De retour à Montréal en 1914, Hébert enseigne le dessin au Conseil des arts et manufactures et en 1917, se voit nommer professeur de dessin à la Commission des Écoles catholiques de Montréal, poste qu'il occupera jusqu'en 1954.

Selon Jean-René Ostiguy[1], l'intérêt d'Hébert pour le post-impressionnisme date de son stage à l'École des Beaux-Arts de Paris, où il se serait pris d'admiration pour Puvis de Chavannes et pour des artistes plus jeunes tels que Maurice Denis et Ker Xavier Roussel. Ostiguy croit qu'Hébert aurait vu le magnifique rideau de scène créé par Roussel pour la Comédie des Champs-Élysées (inaugurée en 1913), et aussi dans ce même théâtre, l'œuvre d'Édouard Vuillard. Toutefois, les premières manifestations du postimpressionnisme chez Adrien Hébert, tout particulièrement l'influence de Cézanne, apparaîtront plus tard – en 1917, dans ses paysages de Percé[2]. Illustrateur de la revue montréalaise avant-gardiste, *Le Nigog*, Hébert aurait été au courant du chaleureux intérêt que son ami, le peintre français Robert Mortier, portait à l'œuvre de Cézanne : Mortier avait publié dans *Le Nigog* un article élogieux sur la ténacité de Cézanne. *L'Enclos, Île Bélair*, qui représente la villa des parents d'Adrien Hébert sur l'Île Bélair dans la Rivière des Mille-Îles, révèle la connaissance qu'avait le peintre des innovations structurales de Cézanne.

1. Jean-René Ostiguy, *Les esthétiques modernes au Québec de 1916 à 1946* (catalogue d'exposition) (Ottawa : Galerie nationale du Canada, 1982), p. 32.
2. Jean-René Ostiguy, *Adrien Hébert : trente ans de son œuvre, 1923–1953* (catalogue d'exposition) (Ottawa : Galerie nationale du Canada, 1971), p. 11.

Randolph S. Hewton

1930

Randolph Stanley Hewton (1888–1960) studied at the Art Association of Montreal under William Brymner from 1903 to 1907; from 1908 to 1910, he studied in Paris at the Académie Julian, and from 1910 to 1913 with Caro Delvaille. A landscape and portrait painter, he had an early interest in the works of Paul Cézanne, such as his *Provençal Landscape*, 1892–1895. *Provençal Landscape* was discussed in depth in the *American Art News* in 1921, and was owned by Dikran K. Kelekian, a respected Paris-based dealer of Near Eastern antiquities. Hewton may have seen the *Loan Exhibition of Impressionist and Post-Impressionist Paintings* at the Metropolitan Museum in 1921, which included many paintings by Cézanne. In his painting *Birches*, Hewton reveals his debt to Cézanne in both motif and brushwork.

14. *Afternoon, Camaret*, c. 1913 / *Après-Midi, Camaret*, v. 1913

15. *Birches*, c. 1921 / *Bouleaux*, v. 1921

Randolph S. Hewton

Randolph Stanley Hewton (1888–1960) a d'abord étudié sous William Brymner à l'Art Association of Montreal (1903–1907), puis à Paris, dans un premier temps à l'Académie Julian (1908–1910) et dans un second avec Caro Delvaille (1910–1913). Portraitiste et paysagiste, il s'est intéressé tôt à l'œuvre de Cézanne comme le démontre son *Paysage provençal* (1892–1895), auquel l'*American Art News* a consacré un article de fond en 1921 et dont avait fait l'acquisition Dikran K. Kelekian, marchand respecté d'antiquités du Proche-Orient installé à Paris. Il est possible que Hewton ait vu la *Loan Exhibition of Impressionist and Post-Impressionist Paintings* au Metropolitan Museum en 1921, laquelle comprenait plusieurs tableaux de Cézanne. À la fois par son motif et sa facture, *Bouleaux* rappelle Cézanne.

Edwin (Headley) Holgate

Beaupré, 1910

Edwin Holgate (1892–1977), like Hewton, was a student of William Brymner at the school of the Art Association of Montreal. He studied in Paris in 1912 at the Grande Chaumière and Julian academies. As it did for Jackson, the First World War strengthened the Post-Impressionist qualities to his work. Early sketches like *Mac Entering Our Bivouac* (1918, The Robert McLaughlin Gallery) show a distinctly stronger handling than his drawings of 1912. Demobilized in 1919, Holgate returned to Montreal where, according to Jackson, he was a prime mover in the Beaver Hall Group in 1920.[1] In mid-November of 1920, he set out again for Paris where from 1921 to 1922, he studied with the Russian-trained painter Adolf Milman. Friendly with James Wilson Morrice, Holgate visited one of Morrice's favourite painting haunts, Concarneau, in the summer of 1921. *Festival of Blue Nets, Concarneau* with its blue tonality touched with areas of bright local colour suggests Morrice's influence.[2]

1. A.Y. Jackson to Eric Brown, 18 January 1921, National Gallery of Canada Archives 7.1-J, cited in Charles C. Hill, *The Group of Seven: Art for a Nation* (Ottawa: National Gallery of Canada, 1995), p. 96.
2. Dennis Reid, *Edwin H. Holgate* (Ottawa: National Gallery of Canada, 1976), p.10.

16. *Festival of Blue Nets, Concarneau*, 1921 / *Fête des filets bleus, Concarneau*, 1921

Edwin (Headley) Holgate

Tel Hewton, Edwin Holgate (1892–1977) a suivi le cours de William Brymner à l'Art Association of Montreal. En 1912, il se retrouve à Paris où il fréquente les académies Julian et de la Grande Chaumière. Comme cela s'est produit pour Jackson, la Première Guerre mondiale a renforcé les qualités postimpressionnistes de son œuvre. Ainsi, des croquis tels *Mac, entrant dans notre bivouac* (1918, The Robert McLaughlin Gallery) dénotent une manière nettement plus forte que celle de ses dessins de 1912. Démobilisé en 1919, Holgate revient à Montréal où, selon Jackson, il joue en 1920[1] un rôle de premier plan au sein du Groupe de Beaver Hall. À la mi-novembre de cette même année, Holgate repart pour Paris où de 1921 à 1922 il étudie avec Adolf Milman, peintre formé en Russie. Ami de James Wilson Morrice, Holgate se rend pendant l'été de 1921 à Concarneau, l'un des endroits où Morrice aimait particulièrement peindre. Par ses tons bleus parsemés de taches aux vives couleurs, *Fête des filets bleus, Concarneau* suggère l'influence de Morrice[2].

1. A.Y. Jackson à Eric Brown, 18 janvier 1921, Archives de la Galerie nationale du Canada 7. I-J, cité dans Charles C. Hill, *Le Groupe des Sept : art d'une nation* (catalogue d'exposition) (Ottawa : Musée des beaux-arts du Canada, 1995), p. 96.
2. Dennis Reid, *Edwin H. Holgate* (Ottawa : Galerie nationale du Canada, 1976), p. 10.

Alexander Young (A.Y.) Jackson

Assisi / Assise, 1912

A.Y. Jackson (1882–1974) was born in Montreal and studied with William Brymner at the Art Association of Montreal. He made three trips to Europe, during the third of which, from about 1910 to 1913, he began to introduce into his work the painterly techniques of late Impressionism. His paintings created in France and Italy show a progression away from tonal effects towards the use of juxtaposed complementary colours, bolder paint handling and an attention to surface design. Jackson believed that the introduction of these effects marked his emergence as a painter.

When he shared a studio with Tom Thomson during the winter of 1914, Jackson told him about Seurat and Pointillism.[1] He would also have described to Thomson the excitement with which such work had been received at the Thirtieth Spring Exhibition in Montreal by the newspapers and public. Jackson felt that Thomson's style changed under his influence – especially when Thomson painted in Petawawa in 1916. Jackson may have shared his findings with Thomson during the autumn and winter of 1914 when Thomson's paintings first began to display a conspicuous "dot" structure.

Jackson's work at the time followed the general drift away from the naturalism of full Impressionism; he had become preoccupied with pictorial structure and with colour. It was only during the First World War, while working as a war artist and possibly under the influence of British art that he would have seen in London that Jackson became a Post-Impressionist. The evidence can be seen in the strong design of paintings such as *Springtime in Picardy*. He said that the change in style occurred because Impressionism did not suit his new subject matter.

1. Interview with A.Y. Jackson by the author, 4 March 1971. Joan Murray, Tom Thomson Papers.

2. A.Y. Jackson, *A Painter's Country: The Autobiography of A.Y. Jackson* (Toronto, Vancouver: Clarke, Irwin & Company Limited, 1958), p. 47.

17. *Springtime in Picardy*, 1919 / *Printemps en Picardie*, 1919

Alexander Young (A.Y.) Jackson

Né à Montréal, A.Y. Jackson (1882–1941) a étudié avec William Brymner à l'Art Association of Montreal. Il a fait trois séjours en Europe et lors du dernier, effectué aux alentours de 1910 à 1913, il a adopté les techniques de l'impressionnisme alors à son déclin. Les tableaux de cette époque créés en France et en Italie laissent voir un éloignement progressif des effets de tons en faveur d'une exploration de la juxtaposition de couleurs complémentaires, d'une utilisation plus crue de la peinture et d'une attention au dessin de surface. Jackson croyait devoir sa naissance comme peintre à l'introduction de ces éléments dans son œuvre.

Jackson a raconté beaucoup plus tard que pendant l'hiver de 1914 il avait fait connaître à Tom Thomson, avec qui il partageait alors un atelier, Seurat et le pointillisme[1]. Il a dû sans doute mentionner les réactions passionnées de la part de la critique et du public aux tableaux pointillistes présentés à la 30e Exposition du printemps de Montréal. Quoiqu'il en soit, Jackson attribue à son influence le changement qui s'est produit dans le style de Thomson – particulièrement lorsque celui-ci peignait à Petawawa en 1916. La communication d'informations à Thomson aurait peut-être eu lieu pendant l'automne et l'hiver de 1914, époque où une structure pointilliste évidente fait son apparition dans la peinture de l'artiste.

Quant à l'œuvre de Jackson, elle s'inscrit dans le mouvement de retrait du naturalisme qui caractérise l'impressionnisme proprement dit. Le peintre s'intéressait surtout à la structure picturale et à la couleur. C'est toutefois seulement au cours de la Première Guerre mondiale que Jackson est devenu postimpressionniste. Ceci se voit dans le dessin fort utilisé pour des tableaux comme *Printemps en Picardie*. La chose se serait produite possiblement sous l'influence de l'art britannique, qu'il aurait certainement vu lorsqu'il travaillait comme artiste de guerre à Londres, en Angleterre. Jackson a attribué son changement de style au fait que l'impressionnisme ne convenait pas à son nouveau sujet.

1. Interview d'A.Y. Jackson par l'auteure, 4 mars 1971. Joan Murray, Tom Thomson Papers.

2. A.Y. Jackson, *A Painter's Country: The Autobiography of A.Y. Jackson* (Toronto, Vancouver : Clarke, Irwin & Company Limited, 1958), p. 47.

Arthur Lismer

c. 1925 / v. 1925

Arthur Lismer (1885–1969) came to Canada in 1911 from Sheffield, England, where he was born, after study at the Sheffield School of Art and at the Académie Royale des Beaux-Arts in Antwerp. He worked at Grip Ltd. from 1911 to 1912 where he met and befriended many artists, among them Tom Thomson and others who with Lismer later became members of the Group of Seven. From his readings of the work of William Morris and the English reformer Edward Carpenter, he developed a holistic vision of art, and from the writings of Clive Bell and Roger Fry, he understood the formal precepts of Post-Impressionism.[1] In his work, about 1916 (influenced by MacDonald who lived nearby), Lismer applied the strong design and sweeping paint application of Post-Impressionism to views of the garden of his house in Thornhill. To these scenes he added a sensitivity to colour that was partially innate, partially influenced by Thomson. The result was a vivid and enthusiastic synthesis of Post-Impressionist style, one with a sense of lyrical intensity.

1. I am indebted for these observations to Charles C. Hill, *The Group of Seven: Art for a Nation*, p. 18.

18. *Winter*, 1920 / *Hiver*, 1920

Arthur Lismer

Né à Sheffield en Angleterre, Arthur Lismer (1885–1969) est venu au Canada en 1911, après des études à la Sheffield School of Art et à l'Académie Royale des Beaux-Arts d'Anvers. De 1911 à 1912, il a travaillé chez Grip Ltd. où il s'est lié d'amitié avec plusieurs artistes, dont Tom Thomson et d'autres peintres qui, comme lui, allaient devenir membres du Groupe des Sept. Ses lectures de l'œuvre de William Morris et de celle du réformateur anglais Edward Carpenter ont déterminé sa vision holistique de l'art tandis que les écrits de Clive Bell et Roger Fry l'ont initié aux préceptes formels du postimpressionnisme[1]. Dans ses tableaux des environs de 1916, réalisés sous l'ascendant de MacDonald qui habitait tout près de chez lui, Lismer conjugue, pour rendre les vues du jardin de sa maison à Thornhill, un dessin incisif et la peinture appliquée à grands coups de pinceau caractéristique du postimpressionnisme. Il y ajoute une sensibilité à la couleur qui semble en partie innée et en partie développée sous l'influence de Thomson. Il s'ensuit un postimpressionnisme brillant et enthousiaste, imprégné d'un lyrisme intense.

1. Je dois ces observations à Charles C. Hill, *Le Groupe des Sept : art d'une nation* (catalogue d'exposition), p. 18.

John Lyman

One of the crucial Canadian pioneers in the birth of modern art in Canada was John Lyman (1886–1967). Like Morrice, whom he knew, Lyman was an expatriot and nomad: he lived in Europe from 1907 until 1931 and thereafter in Canada. Lyman's career echoes that of Morrice. He was first interested in Impressionism, but in 1909, in Paris at the Salon des Indépendents, he saw and was thrilled by the summary intensity of Matisse's *Fontainebleau Forest*.[1] In a letter home the following spring, he mentions other artists whose work interested him, among them Cézanne, Gauguin and van Gogh.[2] In 1910, along with British artist Matthew Smith, he attended the Académie Matisse (see the Appendix for an article he later wrote about Matisse).[3] Lyman recalled Matisse as sober and reflective, with the grave mien of a doctor. Matisse visited his students about once a fortnight and then his criticism usually took the form of a long chat about fundamental principles and qualities;[4] he was "quick to censure the superficial device, the merely decorative abbreviation, the lack of 'density' as he always called it."[5] Lyman also got to see Matisse at work and was fascinated with his way of condensing an incredible wealth of content through many different versions; he later recalled seeing paintings like Matisse's *Red Interior* and *The Dance* at Matisse's house.

At the Académie Matisse, Paris, 1909, second from left. / À l'Académie Matisse, Paris, 1909, deuxième à partir de la gauche

Understandably, because of the influence of Matisse, Lyman's art was indelibly affected. He is probably best known for his Matissean portraits of nude women, but his work was as much about nature and the interiors of places he knew well. In selecting such scenes, Lyman may also have felt the influence of Matisse. As he wrote about Matisse, "Nature was his constant source and reference, no matter how much its particular aspects were modified to suit his general conception."[6]

Lyman's painting of 1912, *Wild Nature (1), Dalesville* (Musée du Québec) seems at first glance to be an art class version of a landscape by Matisse. But the title, *Wild Nature*, suggests other meanings. Lyman's witty balance of formal representation with landscape specifics is overseen here by the recurrent muse of Post-Impressionism. It is a variation on a theme that inspired many Canadian paintings at this particular moment and throughout the century. Like many notable artists of the period, Lyman used simple effects to tackle huge subjects – as he has done in this painting, charmingly and movingly. The forms of the trees resemble large, overblown leaves. The complex planes are rendered with precision, but in a loosely painted way that makes them seem flat, like cut-out patterns. And the individual strokes of paint are applied to create a separate, dynamic network on the painting surface.

Lyman's other works painted between 1912 and 1920

reiterate the same message of cohesive design. All of them deal with the same effects, worked up from a conflation of Matisse's art and what he wrote about it and scenes from Lyman's travels. Each motif, executed often in dark colours, is firmly stated against a richly textured, roughly sketched background. Lyman's explorations had to do with resolving his own painterly problems, but the results are enjoyable in their own right. *Landscape, Bermuda*, c. 1914, for instance, has a silent mood, but seems to encapsulate a typical scene of the island landscape. That it offers a generalized view of Bermuda is reflected in the title the artist gave to the work in 1915: *Bermudian Essay*.[7]

In his compelling *Self-Portrait* and *Portrait of Corinne*, Lyman showed how the rich, sensuous colour of Matisse could be applied to different subjects.

1. John Lyman, "Adieu, Matisse," *Canadian Art* 12, 2 (Winter 1955), p. 44 [reproduced in the Appendix].

2. John Lyman to Frederick Gold Lyman, 20 May 1910, Hedwidge Asselin (ed.), *Inédits de John Lyman* (Montreal: Bibliothèque Nationale du Québec, 1980), quoted in Louise Dompierre, *John Lyman, 1886–1967* (Kingston: Agnes Etherington Art Centre, 1986), p. 29.

3. Lyman appears fourth from the left in a photograph of Matisse among his students at the Académie Matisse, 1909–1910 (see page 13, and detail, page 84). The photograph is in the Archives Matisse, Paris.

4. Lyman, "Adieu, Matisse," pp. 44–45. For a full discussion of Matisse's teaching at the school and related documents, see Jack Flam, *Matisse on Art* (Berkeley: University of California Press, 1995), pp. 44–52.

5. Lyman, "Adieu, Matisse," p. 45.

6. Lyman, "Adieu, Matisse," pp. 45–46.

7. The painting was shown in the Spring Exhibition of the Art Association of Montreal in 1915 (see the John Lyman Accession file on *Landscape, Bermuda*, Curatorial files, National Gallery of Canada, Ottawa).

19. *Café, rue Royal, Paris*, 1909 (?)

20. *Landscape, Bermuda*, c. 1914 / *Paysage, Bermudes*, v. 1914

21. *Portrait of Corinne*, 1919 / *Portrait de Corinne*, 1919

John Lyman

John Lyman (1886–1967), l'un des plus importants pionniers de l'art moderne au Canada, a été, tel Morrice qu'il connaissait, un expatrié et un nomade qui a vécu en Europe de 1907 à 1931 avant de s'établir en permanence au Canada. Sa carrière rappelle d'ailleurs celle de Morrice.

Lyman s'est d'abord intéressé à l'impressionnisme, mais en 1909 il a été électrisé par l'intensité condensée d'un tableau de Matisse, *La forêt de Fontainebleau*[1] exposé au Salon des Indépendants à Paris. Dans une lettre envoyée chez lui le printemps suivant, il mentionne aussi d'autres artistes dont l'œuvre l'a intéressé tels Cézanne, Gauguin et Van Gogh[2]. En 1910, avec l'artiste britannique Matthew Smith, Lyman a fréquenté l'Académie Matisse (on trouvera en Appendice un article qu'il a écrit plus tard sur le peintre français)[3]. Il se rappelait Matisse comme un être sérieux et pensif, ayant la mine grave d'un médecin. Matisse rendait visite à ses étudiants environ une fois tous les quinze jours et sa critique de leur travail prenait la forme d'un long discours sur les principes et les qualités fondamentales[4] de l'art : selon Lyman, le maître « était prompt à condamner les effets superficiels, l'abréviation purement décorative – ce qu'il appelait le manque de « densité[5] ». Lyman, qui a aussi vu Matisse à l'œuvre, était fasciné par sa manière de condenser une richesse de contenu incroyable au fil de nombreuses versions différentes, et il s'est rappelé plus tard avoir vu dans la maison de Matisse des tableaux tels qu'*Intérieur rouge* et *La Danse*.

Que l'influence de Matisse ait eu sur l'art de Lyman un effet indélibile est certes compréhensible. Probablement mieux connu pour ses nus féminins à la Matisse, Lyman a peint, bien aussi souvent, la nature et les intérieurs qui lui étaient familiers. Mais dans le choix de ces scènes, il a peut-être encore subi l'influence du maître. Il a écrit à propos de Matisse : « La nature était sa source constante de référence, peu importe les modifications qu'il apportait à certains de ses aspects pour réaliser sa conception générale[6] ».

À première vue, *Nature sauvage (1), Davisville* (Musée du Québec), que Lyman a peint en 1912, ressemble à un paysage de Matisse réalisé par un élève. Mais le titre, « Nature sauvage », évoque autre chose. La muse récurrente du postimpressionnisme se superpose ici à l'équilibre piquant de la représentation formelle et des détails paysagers. Le thème traité fait l'objet de maints autres tableaux canadiens réalisés au cours de la même période comme tout au long du 20e siècle. Semblable à plusieurs artistes mémorables de l'époque, Lyman utilise de simples effets pour s'attaquer à un large sujet, technique qui dans ce tableau est appliquée de manière charmante et émouvante. La forme des arbres ressemble à d'immenses feuilles. Les plans complexes sont rendus avec précision, mais peints de façon à donner l'impression de patrons plats et découpés, tandis que les coups de pinceau sont appliqués de manière à créer un réseau dynamique indépendant sur la surface du tableau.

Les autres œuvres de Lyman réalisées entre 1912 et 1920 réitèrent l'importance pour le peintre d'un dessin cohésif. Elles mettent à contribution les mêmes effets, lesquels résultent d'une combinaison de l'art de Matisse et de ses écrits sur le sujet, et de scènes de voyages effectués par Lyman. Souvent exécutés dans de sombres couleurs, les motifs se dressent clairement contre un arrière-plan d'une texture riche où la peinture semble appliquée

brusquement et inégalement. Même si Lyman poursuivait dans ces œuvres une solution à certains problèmes picturaux, le résultat n'en est pas moins agréable. Ainsi, *Paysage, Bermudes*, v. 1914, d'humeur silencieuse, semble pourtant bien résumer une scène typique du paysage insulaire. Ce tableau offre une conception généralisée des Bermudes comme l'indique le titre que lui a donné l'artiste en 1915 : « *Bermudian Essay*[7] ».

Dans les fascinants *Autoportrait* et *Portrait de Corinne* Lyman fait voir que la couleur riche et sensuelle de Matisse peut convenir à différent sujets.

1. John Lyman, « Adieu, Matisse », *Canadian Art* 12, 2 (Hiver 1955), p. 44 [reproduit dans l'Appendice].
2. John Lyman à Frederick Gold Lyman, 20 mai 1910, Hedwidge Asselin (éd.) *Inédits de John Lyman* (Montréal : Bibliothèque nationale du Québec, 1980), cité dans Louise Dompierre, *John Lyman, 1886–1967* (catalogue d'exposition) (Kingston : Agnes Etherington Art Centre, 1986), p. 29.
3. Lyman est le quatrième à gauche sur une photo (voir p. 13 et p. 84) de Matisse et de ses étudiants prise à l'Académie Matisse, et datant de 1909–1910. Cette photographie se trouve dans les Archives Matisse, Paris.
4. Lyman, « Adieu, Matisse », p. 44–45. Pour une discussion complète de l'enseignement de Matisse à l'école et autres documents connexes, voir Jack Flam, *Matisse on Art* (Berkeley : University of California Press, 1995), p. 44–52.
5. Lyman, « Adieu, Matisse », p. 45.
6. Lyman, « Adieu, Matisse », p. 45–46.
7. Le tableau faisait partie de l'Exposition de printemps de l'Art Association of Montreal en 1915 (voir le dossier John Lyman sur *Paysage, Bermudes*, Dossier du conservateur, Musée des beaux-arts du Canada, Ottawa).

James Edward Hervey (J.E.H.) MacDonald

c. 1920 / v. 1920

J.E.H. MacDonald (1873–1932), the head designer at the commercial art firm of Grip Ltd. in Toronto from 1907 to 1911, began to paint full-time in 1911. His work was at first influenced by Impressionism, but in January 1913, in the company of Lawren Harris, he saw and was influenced by an exhibition of Scandinavian art at the Albright Art Gallery in Buffalo – particularly by the simplicity of subject matter and presentation.[1] By around 1915, his work (for example, *Garden Flowers*) expressed a general debt to Post-Impressionism, yet at the same time he conveyed a strong design, richly nuanced colour and animation that was very much his own. In this sketch as elsewhere in his painting, simplicity contributes to the result. In general, his paintings are composed of strong diagonals receding into depth and arranged in combinations that stress the flatness of the picture surface to create a paradoxical tension. All of his work is worth close attention for its formal inventiveness and highly expressive qualities.

In 1920, MacDonald became a founding member of the Group of Seven. Paintings like his *Evening, Mongoose Lake*, which was owned by his son Thoreau, indicate the boldness of his handling even in the sketch medium.

1. J.E.H. MacDonald, "Scandinavian Art," *Northward Journal* 18/19 (1980), p. 9 (the text of a talk he gave in 1931), cited in Charles C. Hill, *The Group of Seven: Art for a Nation*, p. 48.

22. *Garden Flowers*, c. 1915 / *Fleurs du jardin*, v. 1915

23. *Evening, Mongoose Lake*, 1920 / *Soir, Lac Mongoose*, 1920

24. *Mist Fantasy, Northland*, 1922 / *Fantaisie brumeuse, Northland*, 1922

James Edward Hervey (J.E.H.) MacDonald

Chef du design de 1907 à 1911 à l'agence torontoise d'art commercial Grip Ltd., J.E.H MacDonald (1873–1932) s'est mis, en 1911, à peindre à plein temps. Son œuvre dénote d'abord l'influence de l'impressionnisme, puis à la suite d'une exposition d'art scandinave qu'il a visitée en janvier 1913 en compagnie de Lawren Harris à l'Albright Art Gallery de Buffalo, celle de l'art nordique dont il a retenu particulièrement la simplicité des motifs et de la présentation[1]. Vers 1915, ses tableaux, tel *Fleurs du jardin*, indiquent l'influence du postimpressionnisme, bien que leurs couleurs richement nuancées et l'animation qui s'en dégage portent la marque personnelle de MacDonald. Dans cette esquisse comme ailleurs dans l'œuvre du peintre, la simplicité renforce le résultat. En général, les tableaux de MacDonald comprennent de fortes lignes diagonales disposées en profondeur dans des agencements qui mettent en valeur la surface plane du tableau de manière à créer une tension paradoxale. L'œuvre entière de MacDonald exige qu'on porte attention à son invention formelle comme à sa grande intensité d'expression.

En 1920, MacDonald a été l'un des membres fondateurs du Groupe des Sept. Des tableaux comme *Soir, Lac Mongoose*, que possédait son fils Thoreau, font état d'une touche vigoureuse, même dans les esquisses.

1. J.E.H. MacDonald, « Scandinavian Art », *Northward Journal 18/19 (1980)*, p. 9 (texte d'une conférence qu'il a donnée en 1931), cité dans Charles C. Hill, *Le Groupe des Sept : art d'une nation* (catalogue d'exposition), p. 48.

Florence H. McGillivray

1930

After study at the Central Ontario School of Art, in 1913 Florence McGillivray (1864–1938) went to Paris to the Académie de la Grande Chaumière. In Paris, she came in contact with Post-Impressionism and in 1913 she exhibited an adventurous figurative painting of a French nun, *Contentment*, at the Salon des Beaux-Arts. Likely in response to seeing the work of van Gogh, she has applied paint boldly in this work using the palette knife, and has massed her colour and drawn a strong black line around forms. Gauguin's influence may be seen in the vague air of piety expressed by the sitter and the diffused symbolism of the subject, but the result in this work is a vivid immediacy. *Contentment* may also show the influence of the artists who surrounded Gauguin known as the School of Pont-Aven: like these artists, McGillivray stressed abstract qualities of line, colour and form.

McGillivray seems to have been immediately accepted in the international community as a talented newcomer. In 1913, she was elected president of the International Art Union, a group that was dissolved when the war started.

She travelled widely in Europe before returning to Canada. In 1914, after visiting Brittany, she was captivated by Venice. The paintings she made in Venice are of conventional subjects, but in these works she explored formal and pictorial complexities and applied paint more assertively so that by 1917 her technique suggested the influence of van Gogh. Her *Canal, Venice*, which was shown in December 1917 at the Small Picture show of the Ontario Society of Artists and in 1918 at the joint Royal Canadian Academy and Ontario Society of Artists exhibition at the Art Gallery of Toronto, is the sketch for one of her strongest works, a major painting of Venice. To this painting of gondolas tied to colourful "paline" with passers-by and gondoliers in the background, she applied formal devices overshadowed, in part, by the human element: the pattern of the gondoliers' hats and standards. This formal order becomes a rational structure that imbues the work with its mix of substance combined with brilliant but fleeting light effects on roughened walls, dark and mysterious doorways and turbulent water.

McGillivray's method of describing forms in massed areas of colour applied with the palette knife was, like that of Thomson and Harris, a first for Canadian art. That she was an important new artist of a particular type can be sensed from the way she conveys, with unusual clarity and drama, the flavour of Venice at sunset. The infectious energy of *Venice* helps us understand why Thomson valued her advice. "She was the only one who understood immediately what I was trying to do," he told a friend. Like him, she forged an independent style characterized by her

fresh use of pattern and colour. Her election to the Ontario Society of Artists in 1917, and to the Society of Women Painters and Sculptors in New York in the same year, was a tribute to her bold vision.

25. *Contentment*, 1913 /*Contentement*, 1913

26. *Canal, Venice*, 1917 / *Canal, Venise*, 1917

27. *Venice*, 1918 (?) / *Venise*, 1918 (?)

Florence H. McGillivray

Après des études à la Central Ontario School of Art, Florence McGillivray (1864-1938) a fréquenté en 1913 l'Académie de la Grande Chaumière à Paris. Pendant son séjour à l'étranger, elle a pris connaissance du postimpressionnisme et en 1913, elle a exposé au Salon des Beaux-Arts un tableau figuratif audacieux, *Contentement*, qui représente une religieuse française. Il semblerait que McGillivray ait vu l'œuvre de Van Gogh avant de le réaliser. En effet, elle y applique la peinture au couteau et avec force, en produisant des masses de couleur et en démarquant les formes au moyen d'une ligne noire tranchée. Par ailleurs, l'air vaguement pieux du modèle et le symbolisme diffus du sujet semblent refléter l'influence de Gauguin. L'impression de vive présence que communique l'œuvre est toutefois typique de McGillivray. *Contentement* dénote peut-être également l'influence des artistes qui entouraient Gauguin à l'École de Pont-Aven : tels ces peintres, McGillivray fait ressortir les qualités abstraites de la ligne, de la couleur et de la forme.

McGillivray paraît avoir été immédiatement acceptée dans la communauté internationale qui voyait en elle une artiste prometteuse. En 1913, elle a été élue présidente de l'International Art Union, laquelle a été dissoute au début de la guerre.

Avant de rentrer au Canada, McGillivray a beaucoup voyagé en Europe, d'abord en 1914 en Bretagne, puis à Venise qui l'a séduite. Ses tableaux de cette ville sont conventionnels par leurs sujets, mais non par leur traitement. En effet, McGillivray y a exploré les complexités formelles et picturales et appliqué la peinture avec beaucoup plus d'audace qu'elle ne l'avait jamais fait, si bien que vers 1917, sa technique rappelait Van Gogh à son plus intense. Présenté en 1918 à l'Art Gallery of Toronto, lors d'une exposition conjointe de l'Académie royale des arts du Canada et de l'Ontario Society of Artists, son *Canal, Venise*, est le croquis d'une de ses œuvres les plus fortes, une peinture importante de Venise. Pour rendre les gondoles liées à un « paline » éclatant, avec en arrière-plan les passants et les gondoliers, elle a utilisé des moyens formels – le patron des chapeaux et des étendards des gondoliers – que l'élément humain tend toutefois à faire oublier. Cet ordre formel impose à l'œuvre une structure rationnelle, où le contenu se mêle aux effets brillants, mais fuyants de la lumière sur des murs rugueux, des portes sombres et mystérieuses et une eau turbulente.

La façon qu'a McGillivray de manipuler la couleur, qu'elle applique tels Thomson et Harris à grands coups de couteau à palette tout en créant des formes, était chose nouvelle au Canada. Que cette artiste ait été une importante nouvelle venue, ayant une niche bien à elle, semble évident par la manière dont elle a su rendre, avec une clarté inhabituelle, le drame que représente Venise au coucher du soleil. L'énergie communicative de *Canal, Venise* nous aide à comprendre la valeur que Thomson accordait à ses conseils. « Elle était la seule personne à comprendre tout de suite ce que j'essayais de faire », a-t-il confié à un ami. Tout comme Thomson, McGillivray s'est forgé un style individuel aux couleurs et aux patrons nouveaux. Son élection en 1917 à l'Ontario Society of Artists, puis à la Society of Women Painters and Sculptors à New York, constitue un hommage à sa vision audacieuse.

(Edward) Middleton Manigault

Edward Middleton Manigault (1887–1922) is a Canadian painter whose art has figured prominently in the Post-Impressionist movement in the United States. He was born in London, Ontario, the son of Edward Manigault, a manager of the London Soap Co. who had emigrated from South Carolina in 1869 after the collapse of the Confederacy. In 1905, Manigault travelled to New York to study at the Art Students League: he became a student and close friend of Kenneth Hayes Miller. In 1913, he was included in the Armory Show. In 1914, he had a very successful one-person show in New York at the newly opened Daniel Gallery (the first of two exhibitions). From the Daniel Gallery, his work entered the broadly based collection of Ferdinand Howald to join paintings by André Derain, Maurice Vlaminck, Juan Gris, and American painters like Theodore Robinson, Maurice Prendergast and Marsden Hartley.[1] Charles Daniel, his regular dealer (Manigault also showed work at the prestigious Montross Gallery in New York),[2] was notable for his discriminating taste at an early date in American art: Daniel showed the work of Peter Blume and Raphael Soyer, among others. He also handled art for Charles Sheeler, John Marin and Jules Pascin.[3] Daniel included in his own collection works by Preston Dickinson and Yasuo Kuniyoshi.[4]

In 1915, Manigault left the United States for service in the First World War: he joined the British expeditionary forces, serving as an ambulance driver with British Army Medical Corps No. 4. After his discharge for medical reasons, he returned to the United States and again started painting. He died in San Francisco of cerebral meningitis. At the time of his death, his work was well regarded: in 1923, for instance, the Metropolitan Museum of Art in New York purchased his painting *Town in France*, along with works by Edgar Degas, James McNeill Whistler, members of the Ashcan School and Rockwell Kent.[5] The art writer Forbes Watson described him as a talented artist who had died prematurely.[6] The two landscapes by Manigault in the Howald collection were described by Watson as showing a decorative tendency that is engaging and delightful. E.R. Hunter discusses his work as fitting in with the fantasies of American painter Arthur B. Davies.[7]

Manigault worked in several media, from the traditional (oil on canvas) to the unusual (glazed ceramic). He had an original eye for colour, structure and form, a sophisticated way with paint and an interest in many subjects, ranging from visionary landscapes, urbanscapes to clown figures. In *Adagio* (Private Collection), shown in the Armory Show and illustrated in the *New York American* for 23 March 1914, Manigault painted six women in various poses seemingly moving to a slow measure.

He was particularly adept at organizing his paintings into structured planes of activity. *Procession*, for instance, depicts a witty and inventive scene in Central Park in New York in which pedestrians, automobiles and horses inhabit discrete spatial locations. At their best, Manigault's figure subjects have painterly verve and ambiguous emotional weight. *The Rocket* demonstrates his attachment to the work of Seurat.

Manigault's painting *New England Town*, reproduced in the *American Art News* of 18 March 1914, shows an astonishing similarity to David Milne's Bronx hillside paintings of 1915. Since both showed at the Armory Exhibition, Milne may have known of Manigault's successful show at the Daniel Galleries in 1914. On the other hand, the resemblance between work by Manigault and Milne may simply point to an interest they shared in the art of Gauguin.

1. Forbes Watson, "American Collections: The Ferdinand Howald Collection," *The arts* 8, 2 (August 1925), pp. 65–95. Today, the collection of Ferdinand Howald (1856–1934) is in the Columbus Museum of Art in Columbus, Ohio.

2. E.R. Hunter, "Edward Middleton Manigault," *Paintings by E. Middleton Manigault, 1887–1922* (West Palm Beach: Norton Gallery of Art, 1963), n.p.

3. Obituary of Charles Daniel, *The New York Times*, 17 May 1971.

4. Picture files, Frick Art Library, New York.

5. *Bulletin of the Metropolitan Museum of Art*, 18 (December 1923), p. 294.

6. Forbes Watson, "American Collections: The Ferdinand Howald Collection," *The arts* 8, 2 (August 1925), p. 86.

7. E.R. Hunter, "Edward Middleton Manigault," *Paintings by E. Middleton Manigault, 1887–1922*.

28. *Procession*, 1911

29. *Mountainous Landscape (or Wide Valley)*, 1913 / *Paysage montagnard (ou Grande vallée)*, 1913

(Edward) Middleton Manigault

Edward Middleton Manigault (1887–1922) est un peintre canadien dont l'œuvre a été longtemps associée au postimpressionnisme américain.

Né à London en Ontario, il était le fils d'Edward Manigault, gérant à la London Soap Co. qui avait émigré de la Caroline du Sud en 1869 après la dissolution des États confédérés. En 1905, Manigault s'est inscrit à l'Art Students League de New York, où il a étudié avec Kenneth Hayes Miller avec qui il s'est lié d'amitié. Il faisait partie des artistes figurant à l'Armory Show en 1913. En 1914, une exposition solo très réussie de ses œuvres avait lieu à la nouvelle Daniel Gallery de New York (la première de deux expositions à cette galerie). De la Daniel Gallery, certains de ses tableaux passèrent à la collection importante de Ferdinand Howald, laquelle comprenait déjà des œuvres d'André Derain, de Maurice Vlaminck, de Juan Gris, et de peintres américains tels que Theodore Robinson, Maurice Prendergast et Marsden Hartley[1]. Charles Daniel, son agent habituel (Manigault a aussi exposé à la prestigieuse Montross Gallery à New York[2]), a su tôt reconnaître le talent chez les artistes américains : c'est lui qui a présenté entre autres Peter Blume et Raphael Soyer. Il a été aussi l'agent de Charles Sheeler, John Marin et Jules Pascin[3], et avait dans sa propre collection des tableaux de Preston Dickson et Yasuo Kuniyoshi[4].

En 1915, Manigault a quitté les États-Unis pour participer à la Première Guerre mondiale : il s'est enrôlé dans les forces expéditionnaires britanniques, et a été conducteur d'ambulance pour le British Army Medical Corps No. 4. Réformé pour raisons médicales, il est retourné aux États-Unis où il s'est remis à peindre. En 1922, une méningite l'emportait à San Francisco. Il jouissait alors d'une excellente réputation. Un an plus tard, en 1923, le Metropolitan Museum of Art à New York faisait l'acquisition de son tableau *Ville en France*, en même temps que d'œuvres d'Edgar Degas, de James McNeill Whistler, de membres de la Ashcan School et de Rockwell Kent[5]. Le critique Forbes Watson voyait en Manigault un artiste doué mort prématurément[6]. Par ailleurs, Watson a observé dans les deux tableaux de Manigault qui se trouvent dans la collection Ferdinand Howald une tendance décorative à la fois engageante et délicieuse. Selon E.R. Hunter, l'œuvre de Manigault cadre bien avec l'imaginaire du peintre américain Arthur B. Davies[7].

Manigault a œuvré dans plusieurs médias, allant de l'orthodoxe (huile sur toile) à l'inusité (céramique émaillée). Il voyait la couleur, la structure et la forme de manière originale, utilisait la peinture avec sophistication, et portait de l'intérêt à plusieurs sujets. Ses motifs vont des paysages fantasques aux paysages urbains en passant par les clowns. Dans *Adagio* (collection privée), exposé à l'Armory Show et reproduit dans le numéro du 23 mars 1914 du *New York American*, six femmes dans des poses diverses semblent se mouvoir lentement.

Ses paysages sont des tours de force de plans parallèles. *Procession*, par exemple, représente une scène amusée et inventive croquée à Central Park à New York : on y note plusieurs plans différents de passants, d'automobiles et de chevaux. Une verve picturale et une ambiguité émotive caractérisent les personnages particulièrement réussis de Manigault. *The Rocket (La Fusée)* témoigne de son affection pour l'œuvre de Seurat.

Par ailleurs, il existe une similarité étonnante entre le *New*

England Town de Manigault, reproduit dans le numéro du 18 mars 1914 de la revue *American Art News*, et les tableaux des collines du Bronx peints par David Milne en 1915. Tous deux faisaient partie de l'Armory Show, et il se peut que Milne ait été au courant de l'exposition prisée de Manigault aux Daniel Galleries en 1914, exposition qui comprenait *New England Town*. Ou encore, la ressemblance entre l'œuvre de Manigault et celle de Milne pourrait simplement indiquer leur intérêt commun pour l'art de Gauguin.

1. Forbes Watson, « American Collections: The Ferdinand Howald Collection », *The arts* 8, 2 (août 1925), p. 65-95. La collection de Ferninand Howald (1856–1934) se trouve aujourd'hui au Columbus Museum of Art, à Columbus dans l'Ohio.

2. E.R. Hunter, « Edward Middleton Manigault », *Paintings by E. Middleton Manigault, 1887–1922* (catalogue d'exposition) (West Palm Beach : Norton Gallery of Art, 1963).

3. Notice nécrologique de Charles Daniel, *The New York Times*, 17 mai 1971.

4. Archives, Frick Art Library, New York.

5. *Bulletin of the Metropolitan Museum of Art*, 18 (décembre 1923), p. 294.

6. Forbes Watson, « American Collections: The Ferdinand Howald Collection », *The arts* 8, 2 (août 1925), p. 86.

7. E.R. Hunter, « Edward Middleton Manigault », *Paintings by E. Middleton Manigault, 1887–1922*.

(Henrietta) Mabel May

1931

One of the students of William Brymner at the Art Association of Montreal, from 1909 to 1912, Henrietta Mabel May (1884–1971) went to Paris in 1912 in the company of Emily Coonan. In 1912, "Henry," as she was called by friends like Anne Savage, travelled to northern France, Belgium, Holland, London, Edinburgh and Glasgow, before returning to Montreal in 1913. She of course came back "radiant," noted Savage, who described her as the leader in the beginning. "She painted with such vigour and strength – gay, rhythmic colour. . . . She loved life painted in the landscape of the Eastern Townships where she built up her swinging happy pictures."[1] *Indian Woman – Oka* (c. 1917) embodied in a small canvas much of what was distinctive about Post-Impressionism: the image recalls references to the "primitive" in the art of Gauguin, particularly his figures of Breton women in *The Vision after the Sermon – Jacob Wrestling the Angel* of 1888. Here, though, May has chosen as her subject a different social group: the First Nations People of Oka. She also may refer to Gauguin's works of this period in her simplification of colour and form and rejection of perspective. Like Gauguin, she believed that the painter should not attempt to imitate nature, but should use it as a stimulus for the imagination.

1. Anne Savage writing about Henrietta Mabel May, Anne Savage Archives, 1896–1971, Concordia University Archives, Montreal, File 6, Public Lectures 2.21.

30. *Indian Woman – Oka*, 1917 / *Femme indienne – Oka*, 1917

(Henrietta) Mabel May

Henrietta Mabel May (1884–1971) a d'abord fréquenté le cours de William Brymner à l'Art Association of Montreal (1909–1912), puis en 1912 s'est rendue à Paris en compagnie d'Emily Coonan. Cette même année, « Henry », comme l'appelaient ses amis dont Anne Savage, a visité le nord de la France, la Belgique et la Hollande, puis Londres, Édimbourg et Glasgow avant de rentrer à Montréal en 1913. Savage, qui la considérait au début comme un chef de file, note qu'elle est revenue « radieuse ». « Elle peignait », écrit-elle, « avec une telle force, une telle vigueur – des couleurs gaies, rythmiques . . . Elle aimait les représentations picturales de la vie dans le paysage des Cantons de l'Est et a réalisé là des tableaux joyeux et pleins d'allant.[1] » *Femme indienne – Oka* (v. 1917) renferme sur une petite toile une vaste quantité d'informations visuelles sur le postimpressionnisme : l'image rappelle le « primitif » dans l'art de Gauguin, en particulier ses femmes bretonnes dans *La Vision après le sermon – La lutte de Jacob avec l'ange*, qui date de 1988. Cependant, May s'intéressait à un groupe social différent, le peuple des Premières Nations à Oka. Mais il n'y a pas que l'image de sa femme indienne qui puisse rappeler le Gauguin de *La Vision;* la simplification de la couleur et de la forme jointe au rejet de la perspective peuvent aussi évoquer le Gauguin de cette période. À l'instar de l'artiste français, May croyait que le peintre ne doit pas chercher à imiter la nature mais y voir simplement le point de départ à son imagination.

1. Propos d'Anne Savage sur Henrietta Mabel May, Archives Anne Savage, 1896–1971, Archives de l'Université Concordia, Montréal, Dossier 6, Conférences publiques 2.21.

David Milne

New York, c. 1909

David Milne (1881–1953), born in Bruce County to Scottish immigrant parents, was one of the great pioneers of modernism in Canadian art. A student in New York at the Art Students League (which played a role in promoting European modernism in American art of the second decade of the century), Milne showed five works at the New York Armory Show in 1913, one of which was *Distorted Tree*, today in the collection of the National Gallery of Canada, Ottawa. Through his art, he pushed actively for the acceptance of Post-Impressionism. *Tree and Grey Rocks* of 1914, for instance, captures in bold strokes of oil paint the play of sunlight on a tree and the seamed face of rock.

Milne saw the work of Cézanne, Gauguin, Matisse and van Gogh in shows at the Little Galleries of the Photo-Secession opened by Alfred Stieglitz at 291 Fifth Avenue, and his oils and works on paper detail the course of his development between 1910 and 1920. His early work in this period reveals the influence of Cézanne and other Post-Impressionists. Milne's broad paint application, restricted palette, and patterned effects pay lively tribute to his masters, though by 1913 the individualism of his style had been set, according to David Silcox.[1]

In 1915, he began to paint hillsides, arranging the pictorial structures of the motif into parallel planes. It was a subject that would continue to interest him throughout his career. From 1916 to 1918 while living at Boston Corners in New York State on the western flank of the Taconic hills, he intensified his formal inventions, drawing silhouetted shapes across a landscape in lines and developing other motifs. In later years, he wrote that one might see a painting like Matisse's *Red Studio* for just a second and be influenced for a lifetime.[2] Milne's many interiors in a restricted colour range, starting around 1914 (one of which is titled *Red*), show the influence of Matisse's *Red Studio*. *Icebox with Kitchen Shelves*, painted in Boston Corners, is proof that Matisse's painting helped Milne discover aesthetic inspiration in the most commonplace domestic objects. Milne wrote that the painting was "merely a collection of observations of shape."[3]

1. David Silcox, *Painting Place: The Life and Work of David B. Milne* (Toronto: University of Toronto Press, 1996), p. 53.
2. Silcox, *Painting Place*, pp. 49 and 387, note 23.
3. David P. Silcox, *London Collects David B. Milne* (Exhibition catalogue) (London: Museum London, 1998).

31. *Blue Interior*, c. 1913 / *Intérieur bleu*, v. 1913

32. *Tree and Grey Rocks*, 1914 / *Arbres et rochers gris*, 1914

33. *Black*, 1914 / *Noir*, 1914

34. *Icebox with Kitchen Shelves*, 1919 / *Glacière avec étagères de cuisine*, 1919

David Milne

Né d'immigrants écossais dans le comté de Bruce en Ontario, David Milne (1881–1953) est l'un des grands pionniers de la modernité en art canadien. En 1913, alors qu'il étudiait à l'Art Students League de New York (institution qui a contribué à promouvoir la modernité européenne dans l'art américain de la deuxième décennie du 20e siècle), il a exposé cinq toiles à l'Armory Show, dont *Arbres déformés*, qui se trouve aujourd'hui dans la collection du Musée des beaux-arts du Canada à Ottawa. Par le biais de son art, il a fait valoir le postimpressionnisme tout en aidant à le faire accepter. Ainsi, *Arbres et rochers gris* (1914) saisit par des touches vigoureuses de peinture à l'huile un événement aussi intrinsèquement pictural que le jeu de la lumière du soleil sur un arbre et la surface veinée d'un rocher.

Milne a vu les tableaux de Cézanne, Gauguin, Matisse et Van Gogh lors d'expositions aux Little Galleries of the Photo-Secession ouvertes par Alfred Stieglitz au 291 Fifth Avenue, et ses huiles et œuvres sur papier révèlent le parcours qu'il a suivi de 1910 à 1920. Les œuvres réalisées au début de cette période dénotent une influence de Cézanne et d'autres postimpressionnistes. Mais si l'ample gestuelle de Milne, sa palette limitée et ses effets décoratifs constituent un vibrant hommage à ses maîtres, le peintre avait néanmoins déjà en 1913 développé son propre style. C'est du moins l'opinion de David Silcox[1].

En 1915 Milne a commencé de peindre à coups de plans parallèles un sujet qu'il allait souvent reprendre à l'avenir : celui des collines. Installé de 1916 à 1918 à Boston Corners, village situé sur le flanc occidental des collines du Taconic dans l'État de New York, il a poussé plus avant ses inventions formelles, dessinant des silhouettes alignées à travers un paysage, et développant aussi d'autres motifs. Il a écrit plus tard qu'il suffisait de voir le temps d'une seconde un tableau tel que *L'Atelier rouge* de Matisse, pour en être influencé pour la vie[2]. Les nombreux intérieurs de Milne (dont un est intitulé *Rouge*), commencés vers 1914 et peints avec une palette restreinte, dénotent l'influence de *L'Atelier rouge* de Matisse. De même, *Glacière et étagères de cuisine*, réalisé à Boston Corners, prouve que la peinture de Matisse a poussé Milne à trouver son inspiration esthétique dans les objets domestiques les plus simples. Milne a remarqué que ce tableau n'était qu'une « simple collection d'observations sur la forme[3] ».

1. David Silcox, *Painting Place: The Life and Work of David B. Milne* (Toronto: University of Toronto Press, 1996), p. 53.

2. Silcox, *Painting Place*, p. 49 et 387, note 23.

3. David P. Silcox, *London Collects David B. Milne* (calatogue d'exposition) (London, Museum London, 1998).

James Wilson Morrice

c. 1891–1900 / v. 1891–1900

The first clear reference in Canadian art to the new developments occurred with the work of James Wilson Morrice (1865–1924) around 1903. During the 1890s while living in Europe, first in London, then in 1892 in Paris, his paintings had a "pleasing soft grey tone," according to critics.[1] Indeed, Morrice's paintings of the period are distinguished by their restrained colour and tonal organization. At this time, he met several painters from the United States, among them Maurice Prendergast, who likely spurred his desire for freedom from the limitations of conventional painting. In 1896, he began using small wood panels as surfaces for oil sketches painted on-the-spot. At this early moment, his work recalled that of James McNeill Whistler or perhaps the English painter Albert Sickert – like these artists, he revelled in his preference for the evocative over the representational, using a greyed range of colours. A visit to Quebec in 1897 where he met Canadian Impressionist Maurice Cullen, however, prompted him to lighten his palette and in turn become more fascinated with fleeting effects of light and atmosphere, the hallmarks of Impressionist painting.

Around 1903, he significantly brightened his colour and began to use more of a Pointillist technique in which he juxtaposed rectangular brush strokes. It was at this point that his work shifted from Impressionism to Post-Impressionism, according to John O'Brian.[2] *Venice, Looking Out over the Lagoon* (Montreal Museum of Fine Arts), for instance, presents a vision of pulsating sky and water rendered in combinations of pink, yellow and pale green. Its strong design is enhanced by its clearly visible brush strokes.

The mood of this painting is one of dreamy suspension. The people, standing or seated, are divided by the long horizontals of the design and the gondola and sailboat that lie becalmed in the water express an almost magical quality of stillness and reverie. Morrice's firm grounding in traditional art practices shows in his classically solid organization and his orchestration of light and dark.

Morrice's haunting vision was peculiar to him even among the Post-Impressionists whose work he drew upon for his methods; however, he was probably most influenced by Gauguin whose work was brought to his attention by Roderic O'Conor, the expatriate Irish painter who had known both Gauguin and van Gogh.[3] Morrice would have found in the work of Gauguin many affinities, particularly stylistic ones, and he perhaps learned from Gauguin ways of strengthening his composition and colour. The example of Gauguin may also have influenced him to thin out the heavily layered pigment of his earlier work. But the feeling of spiritual distance in Morrice's work is at odds with Gauguin's expansive exoticism. O'Brian links Morrice with the group known as the Nabis (Hebrew for "prophets"), which formed in 1889 and counted among its members Pierre Bonnard

and Edouard Vuillard. These "Intimists," as they are called, painted sequestered interiors that reverberated with quiet, indefinable dramas. Vuillard, in particular, created an almost palpable sense of atmosphere with his densely layered patterns and textures. As O'Brian points out, a sense of intimacy suffused Morrice's work. Morrice himself praised the work of Bonnard, writing a friend in 1911 that Bonnard was the best man in Paris, since the death of Gauguin.[4] Like that of Bonnard, Morrice's work shows a preference for flat, decorative colour combined with an interest in modern subjects. His depiction of figures promenading by a bridge conjures associations to Japanese prints, much admired by Bonnard and the artistic avant-garde.

Critics often discuss Morrice's technical proficiency. The handling in his *pochades*, or little sketches, is broad and vigorous. Like his canvases, they are highly decorative, vigorously combining three-dimensional space and two-dimensional design.

Morrice's two trips to Tangier in Morocco profoundly affected his work. On his first visit, in January 1912, he began to introduce brighter colour into his paintings and to use Moroccan subjects. His second trip, from December of 1912 to February of 1913, coincided with a sojourn by Henri Matisse, who later in his work conveyed to perfection the "utter calm" he found there.[5] The two met and would likely have exchanged ideas about art. Aspects of Morrice's paintings following his visit to Tangier and up to the very last paintings of his career, particularly their decorative quality and the luminous, trancelike feeling of space and time (for example, *Afternoon, Tunis*, *Village Street, West Indies* and *Quebec Farmhouse*) may show Matisse's influence. Other works of this period, like *Café El Pasajo*, c.1915 (National Gallery of Canada, Ottawa), use a compositional motif very popular with Matisse: the view seen through a window. *Nude with a Feather*, c.1909–1913 (Montreal Museum of Fine Arts) also recalls portraits by Matisse, particularly in its background and its handling, but Morrice's work is notable for its informal, close-cropped treatment of its subject. The suggestion that the nude is brushing powder on her lush body has a powerful but subtle eroticism. "The artist with the delicate eye," Matisse called Morrice.[6]

In other works such as his *North African Town*, Morrice took a brave new tack on the representation of nature, conveying the dazzling light and heat of Tangier with a narrow range of tans, greys and pinks touched in spots with red and green, the whole set off by intense blue skies. North Africa encouraged him to summarize the essence of a subject and adopt more vivid hues. Morrice's individuality is in his formal sense of composition and decorative patterning, the latter his heritage from the Nabis.

1. "Water Colours: The Annual Spring Exhibition," Toronto *Star*, 20 April 1881, quoted in Nicole Cloutier, "The Gentleman Painter," *James Wilson Morrice 1865–1924* (Montreal: Montreal Museum of Fine Arts, 1985).
2. John O'Brian, "Morrice's Pleasures (1900–1914)," in Cloutier, *James Wilson Morrice 1865–1924* (Montreal: Montreal Museum of Fine Arts, 1985), p. 93.
3. O'Brian, *James Wilson Morrice*, p. 93.
4. Morrice to Edmund Morris, Edmund Morris Letterbooks, E.P. Taylor Art Reference Library Archives, Art Gallery of Ontario, Toronto.
5. Matisse's second trip to Morocco lasted from late September until mid-February 1913 (Xavier Girard, *Matisse: The Wonder of Color* [New York: Harry N. Abrams, Inc., 1993], p. 79).
6. Henri Matisse, letter to Armand Dayot [late 1925], *James Wilson Morrice* (Paris: Galleries Simonson, 1926), pp. 6–7.

35. *North African Town*, c. 1912–1913 / *Ville d'Afrique du Nord*, v. 1912–1913

36. *View of a North African Town*, c. 1912–1913 / *Vue d' une ville d' Afrique du Nord*, v. 1912–1913

37. *Afternoon, Tunis*, c. 1914 / *L'après-midi à Tunis*, v. 1914

38. *Village Street, West Indies*, c. 1915–1919 / *Rue d’ un village aux Antilles*, v. 1915–1919

39. *Quebec Farmhouse*, c. 1921 / *Maison de ferme québécoise*, v. 1921

James Wilson Morrice

On doit à l'œuvre de James Wilson Morrice (1865–1924) la première allusion évidente aux nouveaux développements qui allaient se produire dans l'art canadien. La chose a eu lieu vers 1903. Les critiques ont remarqué[1] que dans les années 1890, alors qu'il vivait en Europe – à Londres d'abord, puis en 1892 à Paris – Morrice utilisait dans sa peinture « un ton gris doux et plaisant », apparenté au tonalisme. En effet, l'œuvre de Morrice durant ce temps se caractérise par sa palette restreinte et son organisation tonale. Or, à cette époque, le peintre a rencontré plusieurs artistes américains, dont Maurice Prendergast, qui l'ont vraisemblablement encouragé à se libérer des conventions picturales restrictives. En 1896, il a commencé à utiliser de petits panneaux de bois pour peindre en plein air ses croquis à l'huile. Ces œuvres des débuts évoquent les tableaux de James McNeill Whistler ou peut-être ceux du peintre anglais Albert Sickert. Au réel, Morrice préférait l'évocatif qu'il aimait rendre dans un registre de tons gris, bien qu'une visite au Québec en 1897, où il a rencontré l'impressionniste canadien Maurice Cullen, l'ait amené à alléger sa palette.

Vers 1903, Morrice s'est mis à utiliser des couleurs plus vives et un pointillisme auquel il juxtaposait des touches rectangulaires : c'est à cette époque que, selon John O'Brian[2], il est devenu postimpressionniste. *Venise, vue à travers la lagune* (Musée des beaux-arts de Montréal) présente ainsi, dans des tons de rose, jaune et vert pâle, un paysage vibrant de ciel et d'eau dans lequel un dessin fort se joint à des traits de pinceau affirmés.

Ce tableau donne l'impression que tout est en suspens, comme dans un songe. Les personnages assis ou debout, séparés par les plans horizontaux, et la gondole et le voilier, encalminés sur l'eau, produisent un effet presque magique de tranquillité et de rêverie. La formation classique de Morrice se révèle dans la solide organisation des éléments et l'orchestration des ombres et de la lumière.

Cette vision obsédante était propre à Morrice; il ne la tenait pas des postimpressionnistes desquels, toutefois, il a probablement tiré certaines de ses méthodes. Sans doute a-t-il été particulièrement intéressé par l'œuvre de Gauguin que lui avait révélée un peintre irlandais expatrié, Roderic O'Conor, qui avait bien connu Gauguin et Van Gogh[3]. Morrice se serait trouvé plusieurs affinités avec Gauguin, sur le plan stylistique en particulier, et il aurait peut-être appris de Gauguin des moyens de renforcer sa couleur et sa composition. Il aurait aussi découvert une façon de diluer la lourde pigmentation de ses œuvres antérieures. Mais l'exotisme expansif de Gauguin n'aurait pu convenir à Morrice comme le démontrent leur peintures respectives où se révèle une réelle distance spirituelle. O'Brian voit un lien entre Morrice et les Nabis (le mot hébreu pour « prophètes »), groupe formé en 1889 et incluant entre autres Pierre Bonnard et Édouard Vuillard. Ces « intimistes », comme on les appelle, peignaient des intérieurs fermés, lourds de drames silencieux et indéfinissables. Vuillard, tout particulièrement, a su créer, avec ses patrons et ses textures d'une riche densité, une atmosphère presque palpable. Selon O'Brian, un sentiment d'intimité semblable se dégage de l'œuvre de Morrice. Ce dernier a fait l'éloge de Bonnard dans une lettre de 1911 à un ami, où il affirme que Bonnard était le meilleur peintre à Paris depuis la mort de Gauguin[4]. Or, tel Bonnard, Morrice a une préférence pour la couleur

décorative platement étalée ainsi qu'un intérêt pour les sujets modernes. On peut voir dans ses personnages se promenant le long d'un pont une référence aux estampes japonaises qui faisaient l'admiration de Bonnard et de l'avant-garde artistique.

Les critiques s'attachent souvent à la compétence technique de Morrice, qui réalise ses pochades, ou petites esquisses, avec vigueur. Tout comme ses toiles, celles-ci sont hautement décoratives, et frappent le spectateur à la fois par leur espace tridimensionnel et leur dessin bidimensionnel.

On fait souvent état des deux voyages de Morrice à Tanger au Maroc. Durant son premier voyage en janvier 1912, il s'est mis à peindre avec des couleurs plus vives et à utiliser des sujets marocains. Durant son deuxième voyage, de décembre 1912 à février 1913, il s'est trouvé à Tanger en même temps qu'Henri Matisse, qui a su rendre plus tard à la perfection le calme absolu[5] de l'endroit. Les deux artistes ont pu échanger des idées sur l'art. Certains tableaux de Morrice, dont *L'après-midi à Tunis*, *Rue d'un village aux Antilles* et *Maison de ferme québécoise*, dénotent peut-être l'influence de Matisse, particulièrement pour ce qui est de leurs qualités décoratives et de leur rapport lumineux et quasi extatique face à l'espace/temps – qualités qui ressortent non seulement à la suite du séjour de Morrice à Tanger mais se retrouvent également plus tard dans son art, en fait jusque dans ses toutes dernières œuvres. Le motif de composition d'autres tableaux de cette période, par exemple *Café El Pasajo*, v. 1915 (Musée des beaux-arts du Canada, Ottawa), rappelle aussi Matisse, en l'occurrence par son motif d'une fenêtre s'ouvrant sur une vue, thème constant chez le peintre français. *Femme au peignoir rouge*, vers 1909–1913 (Musée des beaux-arts de Montréal) évoque le Matisse des portraits, en partie à cause de son arrière-plan et de son traitement, encore que Morrice peigne son sujet de très près et de manière familière. Le fait que la femme nue semble saupoudrer son corps bien en chair contient un érotisme puissant mais subtil. « L'artiste à l'œil délicat », a dit Matisse de Morrice.

Dans d'autres tableaux comme *Ville d'Afrique du Nord*, Morrice a essayé une nouvelle et audacieuse tactique pour représenter la nature. Il a rendu la chaleur et la lumière aveuglante de Tanger à l'aide d'une palette restreinte d'ocres, de gris et de roses parsemés de rouge et de vert, le tout contre un ciel d'un bleu intense. L'Afrique du Nord l'a poussé à rendre la nature intime d'un sujet et à adopter des couleurs plus vives. L'essence de Morris se trouve dans son sens formel de la composition et dans ses éléments décoratifs hérité des Nabis.

1. « Water Colours: The Annual Spring Exhibition », *Star* de Toronto, 20 avril 1881, cité dans Nicole Cloutier, « The Gentleman Painter », *James Wilson Morrice 1865–1924* (catalogue d'exposition) (Montréal : Musée des beaux-arts de Montréal, 1985).

2. John O'Brian, « Morrice's Pleasures (1900–1914) », dans Cloutier, *James Wilson Morrice 1865–1924* (catalogue d'exposition) (Montréal : Musée des beaux-arts de Montréal, 1985).

3. O'Brian, *James Wilson Morrice*, p. 93.

4. Morrice à Edmund Morris, Edmund Morris Letterbooks, Archives, E.P. Taylor Art Reference Library, Musée des beaux-arts de l'Ontario, Toronto.

5. Le second voyage de Matisse au Maroc a eu lieu de la fin septembre 1912 à la mi-février 1913 [Xavier Girard, *Matisse: The Wonder of Color* (New York : Harry N. Abrams, Inc., 1993), p. 79.]

6. Henri Matisse, lettre à Armand Dayot (tard en 1925, *James Wilson Morrice* (Paris : Galeries Simonson, 1926), p. 6–7.

Albert Henry (A.H.) Robinson

1920s / Less années 1920

Concentrating on the enrichment of painting through elegant pattern and animated colour to create sensually gratifying effect, Albert Robinson lends a special quality to the history of Canadian art. After study with Impressionist painter John S. Gordon at the Hamilton Art School (1901–1903), Robinson (1881–1956) attended the Académie Julian and École des Beaux-Arts in Paris from 1903 to 1906. He spent the summers of 1904 and 1905 travelling and painting in Normandy with the English painter Thomas William Marshall. In 1908 he settled in Montreal where he associated with William Brymner and Impressionist Maurice Cullen. In 1911, a breakthrough came about in his work when he travelled to France with A.Y. Jackson. Together with Jackson he visited Brittany and St. Malo, and then travelled back to Canada in 1912. During the First World War, he spent four years as a munitions inspector for Dominion Copper Products at Longue Pointe, Quebec, afterwards returning to his career as an artist with increased vigour. The four years away from painting had consolidated his ambition. Now his work gained a new brilliancy of colour and strength of design: he became a pioneer of Post-Impressionism, rethinking conventional forms. *Noontime, Longue Pointe Village* shows Robinson's gift for paring form to essentials and for uniting his design with a lyrical sense of colour. In this painting, he applied pink to the central telephone pole, a rooftop and the shadow on the snow. He continued to paint, creating a dynamic body of work inspired by visits to various areas in Quebec, often accompanied by Jackson and Holgate.

40. *Noontime, Longue Pointe Village*, 1919 / *Midi, village de Longue Pointe*, 1919

Albert Henry (A.H.) Robinson

Par l'agréable sensation de sensualité qui émane de ses tableaux, sensation due à leurs décorations élégantes et leur couleur animée, Albert Robinson (1881–1956) a apporté une contribution spéciale à l'histoire de l'art canadien. Après des études auprès du peintre impressionniste John S. Gordon de l'Hamilton Art School (1901–1903), il a fréquenté l'Académie Julian et l'École des Beaux-Arts à Paris (1903–1906), voyageant et peignant en Normandie pendant les étés de 1904 et 1905 en compagnie du peintre anglais Thomas William Marshall. En 1908, il s'est établi à Montréal, où il s'est associé avec William Brymner et l'impressionniste Maurice Cullen. En 1911, son art se transforme à la suite d'un voyage en France avec A.Y. Jackson. Ensemble ils ont visité la Bretagne et St-Malo, pour revenir au Canada en 1912. Pendant la Première Guerre mondiale, Robinson a passé quatre ans comme inspecteur des munitions au Dominion Copper Products à Longue Pointe au Québec, pour ensuite retourner à la peinture avec une vigueur accrue. Les quatre années passées loin de ses pinceaux ont raffermi son ambition. Son œuvre fait preuve désormais de couleurs plus éclatantes et d'une nouvelle force dans le dessin : il est devenu un pionnier du postimpressionnisme, repensant les formes conventionnelles. *Midi, village de Longue Pointe* montre le don qu'il avait pour réduire la forme à ses composantes essentielles et unifier le tout par le lyrisme de sa couleur. Dans ce tableau, Robinson a peint en rose le poteau téléphonique central, un toit et l'ombre sur la neige. Il a continué de peindre, créant un ensemble d'œuvres dynamiques en installant son chevalet à divers endroits au Québec, souvent en compagnie de Jackson et d'Holgate.

Anne Savage

c. 1920 / v. 1920

From 1914 to 1918, Anne Savage (1896–1971) studied at the Art Association of Montreal with William Brymner and Impressionist Maurice Cullen, and then from 1919 to 1920 at the Minneapolis School of Art. She was a member of the Beaver Hall Group. *Untitled (Canal)*, c. 1915–1918, was probably painted during her time at the Art Association: both the paint application and subject identify it with her student days. Charles C. Hill points out that the painting recalls Cullen and may indicate that Cullen, who often worked on students' sketches, corrected the painting.[1] Her painting of Lake Wonish in the Laurentians, an early work, is boldly painted, depicting in shades of purple a view of willowy tree trunks capped by swirls of foliage.[2] Her use of a thin surface of paint and notational style suggests the influence of the earlier work of Morrice or of Post-Impressionists whom she had discovered around this time.

Her 1919 portrait of William Brymner, a tribute to this broad-minded man who was sympathetic to new developments in art, suggests both what she learned from him and what he was like as a person. With its bold execution, it illustrates Savage's energy and lively insight into her subject. Brymner's depiction has a sardonic air, partly the result of the monocle she shows him wearing. Savage recalled him as a wit (see the Appendix) and her thoughtful painting strikes just the right note.

1. See Charles C. Hill, Anne Savage Accession file, Curatorial files, National Gallery of Canada, Ottawa. Hill refers to an interview of Anne Savage by A. Calvin, 1967, in the Anne Savage Papers, Concordia University, file 73, 18.3, p. 22 in which Savage mentions that Cullen helped give her a feeling for the big contour.
2. Reproduced in Anne McDougall, *Anne Savage: The Story of a Canadian Painter* (Montreal: Harvest House, 1977).

41. *Untitled (Canal)*, c. 1915–1918 / *Sans titre (Canal)*, v. 1915–1918

42. *Portrait of William Brymner*, 1919 / *Portrait de William Brymner*, 1919

Anne Savage

Membre du Groupe de Beaver Hall, Anne Savage (1886–1971) a d'abord étudié avec William Brymner et l'impressionniste Maurice Cullen à l'Art Association of Montreal (1914–1918), puis à la Minneapolis School of Art (1919–1920). Comme le suggèrent le motif du tableau et la manière d'appliquer la peinture, *Sans titre (Canal)*, v. 1915–1918, représente probablement un travail d'élève réalisé à l'Art Association. Selon Charles C. Hill, cette toile rappelle l'esthétique de Cullen et indiquerait peut-être que Cullen, qui retravaillait souvent les croquis des étudiants, aurait corrigé le tableau[1]. Dans sa toile du Lac Wonish dans les Laurentides, une œuvre de jeunesse, elle applique la peinture hardiment, combinant des tons de violet avec des troncs d'arbre élancés couronnés de feuilles tourbillonnantes[2]. Savage emploie ici une fine couche de peinture et un style de notations évocateur du premier Morrice ou encore de postimpressionnistes qu'elle aurait découverts à l'époque. Son portrait de Brymner (1919), qui constitue un hommage à cet homme aux idées larges, ouvert aux nouvelles tendances artistiques, évoque à la fois ce que Savage a appris de Brymner et ce que Brymner était en tant qu'être humain. La facture vigoureuse et énergique de l'œuvre et la perspicacité avec laquelle Savage a pénétré son sujet captivent l'attention du spectateur. Brymner a un air sardonique, dû en partie à son monocle. Savage se rappelait Brymner comme un homme d'esprit (voir Appendice : Souvenirs et témoignages) et le portrait réfléchi qu'elle a fait de lui sonne juste.

1. Voir Charles C. Hill, Anne Savage, Dossier du conservateur, Musée des beaux-arts du Canada, Ottawa. Hill fait référence à une entrevue d'Anne Savage par A. Calvin, 1967, Documents Anne Savage, Université Concordia, dossier 73, 18.3, p. 22; Savage y mentionne l'aide de Cullen concernant le grand contour.
2. Reproduit dans Anne McDougall, *Anne Savage: The Story of a Canadian Painter* (Montreal : Harvest House, 1977)

Thomas John (Tom) Thomson

1916 (?)

The name Tom Thomson (1877–1917) conjures up a romantic image of the mysterious North for many Canadians who view him as the archetypal Canadian painter. His work (some forty canvases and four hundred sketches) in his five-year career consisted, by and large, of joyous encomiums to nature. His development was towards relaxed, brilliant handling of paint; at his best he disposes trees and bushes like notes in a finely phrased tune and his patterns interlock in intricate counterpoint.

Thomson's depictions of the woods of his favourite painting place, Ontario's Algonquin Park, show a landscape of crossing forms and lines. The result is never claustrophobic because there is always a touch of sky or lake to open up the view. His was a traditional way of painting, but not heavy-handed: his works have an unassuming air, even as they overwhelm with their sumptuous colour.

Thomson's style as a mature painter falls between late Impressionism and Post-Impressionism. His knowledge of Post-Impressionism derived partially from his friendship with A.Y. Jackson, whom he met in November 1913 while still a commercial artist. Jackson, who had been in France from 1911 to 1913, told Thomson about Pointillism and Seurat,[1] and described to Thomson the "clean cut dots" of colour[2] during the period in January and February of 1914 when the two shared Studio One in the Studio Building. Jackson likely presented Thomson with a vast array of ideas, fuelling Thomson's ambition with his impressive precedents: in a sketch and two canvases Thomson painted during that winter, *Moonlight Nocturne*, *Moonlight, Early Evening* (National Gallery of Canada, Ottawa) and *The Morning Cloud*, he rose to new heights. In these rather elegant works, Thomson created dense surface patterns composed of strokes of pastel colour producing effects that are both optically brilliant and gently vibrating. Thomson's homage to European art in these paintings indicates his leap into a new pictorial world. Among those who encouraged him in his shift to Post-Impressionism were Lawren Harris and Florence McGillivray. The influence of Harris's work of 1915 and 1916 can be seen in some of Thomson's studio paintings of the winters of 1915–1916 and 1916–1917, which have a similar square structure and broad brushwork. McGillivray visited him in the studio during the winter of 1916–1917 and would have given Thomson's paintings thoughtful attention since in her own work from 1913 on she was using a broad application, one in which the palette knife played a key role. Thomson found in her a kindred spirit – she was sympathetic and understanding: he later told a friend how much her visit pleased him and stored her calling card and an invitation to

a show of 1917 in his paintbox, where they were found after his death.

Thomson painted like an attentive man in a hurry, using the brush with confidence and employing a sizable vocabulary of delicate strokes and broad swatches of colour. In his small sketches, he sought a summary effect attained with quick thin lines, single and grouped. His vision is marked by his sense of keen observation of the effects of changing light and weather. He amply conveyed his affection for the northern Ontario landscape, using thick impasto and complementary colour mixtures. In *Autumn Trees, Algonquin Park*, for instance, he set off brilliant crimson, orange and yellow leaves by placing them against grey and green – but always, as he told a friend, he left light at the top, a touch of sky, to open up the space. In *Nocturne*, a two-sided panel he painted during the autumn of 1916, Thomson painted an autumn scene on a grey day, then on the reverse, delineated the effect upon the snow of a thaw in the woods, likely the season's first snowfall.

From an early date, Thomson learned to simplify forms for powerful effect, sometimes to the point of being called Cubist by his friends, such as A.Y. Jackson and F.H. Varley, both of whom applied the word to him in letters written during the autumn of 1914.[3] In fact, Thomson with his high-keyed colour, notational style and strong design is a sibling to the Fauves. Possibly, too, he had read or heard about Cloisonnism. The term describes the method evolved by the French artists Louis Anquetin and Émile Bernard. It was based on the design of Japanese prints with the addition of elements from medieval stained glass and the exploitation of flat areas of colour as in *cloisonné* enamelling. Thomson created an effect of stained glass in his painting *The Jack Pine* (National Gallery of Canada, Ottawa), though likely the reference derived more from his knowledge of the stained glass of Louis Comfort Tiffany than from medieval art. Thomson's real contribution to Canadian Post-Impressionism lies in his interpretation of the northern landscape and his feeling for the structure of the land. Later, members of the Group of Seven recall finding in Thomson's paintings of 1912 the first traces of the subject matter that would become so indelibly identified with their work.

1. Interview with A.Y. Jackson by the author, 4 March 1971. Joan Murray, Tom Thomson Papers.
2. Interview with Jackson.
3. Letter from A.Y. Jackson, 13 October 1914, and letter from F.H. Varley, both to Dr. J.M. MacCallum, October 1914, MacCallum Correspondence, National Gallery of Canada Archives.

43. *Phantom Tent*, c. 1915 / *Tente fantôme*, v. 1915

44. *Autumn Trees, Algonquin Park*, c. 1915–1916 / *Arbres en automne, parc Algonquin*, v. 1915–1916

45. *Autumn Birches*, c. 1916 / *Bouleaux en automne*, v. 1916

46. *Nocturne*, c. 1916 / *Nocturne*, v. 1915

46. Verso of *Nocturne*, c. 1916 / Verso de *Nocturne*, v. 1916

47. *The Drive*, c. 1916 / *La Drave*, v. 1916

Thomas John (Tom) Thomson

Pour les nombreux Canadiens qui voient en Thomson (1877–1917) l'archétype du peintre canadien, la seule évocation de son nom fait aussitôt surgir une image romantique du Nord mystérieux. Sa peinture (quelque 40 toiles et 400 esquisses réalisées en l'espace de cinq ans) est dans l'ensemble une joyeuse célébration de la nature. Son évolution témoigne d'une recherche en vue d'une peinture détendue et éclatante; à son mieux, l'artiste dispose les arbres et les taillis comme autant de notes dans une belle phrase musicale. Son agencement des éléments ressemble à un savant contrepoint.

Ce que Thomson a vu dans la forêt du parc Algonquin en Ontario, endroit où il aimait particulièrement peindre, ressemblait à un espace sillonné d'objets, apparaissant souvent en diagonale. Le résultat n'est jamais claustrophobique car toujours la toile recèle un coin de lac ou de ciel. Thomson peignait de façon traditionnelle mais non sans grâce. Il n'existe aucune prétention dans ses toiles, même lorsque leur couleur somptueuse nous plonge dans l'étonnement.

Le style de maturité de Thomson se situe entre le néo-impressionnisme et le postimpressionnisme. Le peintre tenait sa connaissance de celui-ci grâce en partie à A.Y. Jackson, qu'il avait rencontré en novembre 1913 alors qu'il était artiste commercial, et avec qui il s'était lié d'amitié. Jackson, qui avait vécu en France de 1911 à 1913, a rapporté plus tard qu'il avait entretenu Thomson du pointillisme et de Seurat[1], et qu'il se rappelait lui avoir décrit les « points précis » de couleur[2] qui caractérisaient le pointillisme. La chose avait eu lieu de janvier à février 1914 alors que les deux artistes partageaient le Studio n° 1 du Studio Building. Vraisemblablement Jackson a présenté à Thomson un vaste assortiment d'idées, de projets ambitieux et de précédents impressionnants, car dans une esquisse et deux toiles exécutées durant cet hiver particulier, *Clair de lune – nocturne*, *Clair de lune* et *Tôt dans la soirée* (Musée des beaux-arts du Canada, Ottawa), ainsi que dans *Le Nuage matinal*, Thomson a atteint de nouveaux sommets. Dans ces œuvres plutôt élégantes, le peintre a créé des plans denses formés de traits pastel, produisant un effet éclatant et légèrement vibratoire. Réalisées en hommage à l'art européen, ces œuvres devaient représenter le saut du peintre dans un nouvel univers pictural, voie dans laquelle l'ont encouragé entre autres Lawren Harris et Florence McGillivray. Certains des tableaux de Thomson exécutés en atelier pendant les hivers de 1915–1916 et 1916–1917 indiquent d'ailleurs, par leur structure carrée et leurs larges traits de brosse, que le peintre a tenté d'émuler l'œuvre du Harris de 1915 et 1916. D'autre part, au cours d'une visite à l'atelier de Thomson pendant cette période, McGillivray aurait regardé les tableaux de son collègue avec une attention et une considération particulières car depuis 1913 elle utilisait elle-même une technique faite de larges gestes, où le couteau à palette jouait un rôle important. Comme Thomson devait le confier plus tard à un ami, McGillivray lui a paru sympathique et compréhensive. Sa visite lui a fait plaisir et il a gardé sa carte de visite et son carton d'invitation à une exposition de 1917. On les a découverts après sa mort dans sa boîte de couleurs.

Thomson peignait tel un homme attentif mais pressé, utilisant le pinceau avec assurance et un vocabulaire considérable de traits délicats et de larges taches de couleur. Dans ses petits

croquis, de minces lignes brièvement tracées, seules ou groupées, lui permettent d'atteindre le condensé recherché. Un sens aigu de l'observation et des variations de la lumière et du temps caractérisent sa vision. Il a amplement exprimé son affection pour le paysage du Nord ontarien, qu'il a rendu au moyen d'un épais empâtement et de mélanges de couleurs complémentaires. Dans *Arbres en automne, parc Algonquin*, il fait contraster des feuilles de tons éclatants de rouge, d'orange et de jaune avec du gris et du vert, laissant de la place dans le haut de la toile, ainsi qu'il le faisait toujours dans ses tableaux (comme il l'avait dit à un ami), à un coin de ciel pour ouvrir l'espace. Dans *Nocturne*, un panneau à deux faces créé à l'automne de 1916, Thomson a peint un paysage d'automne au ciel couvert, puis – au dos – il a illustré l'effet de dégel dans la forêt, au moyen de traces laissées dans la neige, vraisemblablement la première chute de neige de la saison.

Tôt dans sa carrière, Thomson a tiré un effet puissant de la simplification des formes, au point parfois d'être qualifié de « cubiste » par certains de ses amis. A.Y. Jackson et F.H. Harley ont ainsi tous deux utilisé ce terme à son propos dans des lettres de l'automne 1914[3]. En fait, la couleur rutilante de Thomson, son style de notations et sa ligne vigoureuse l'apparentent davantage au fauvisme. Il a pu aussi s'inspirer du « cloisonnisme » développé par les artistes français Louis Anquetin et Émile Bernard, et fondé sur l'estampe japonaise additionnée d'éléments de vitraux médiévaux et de zones plates de couleur comme dans le glaçage dit cloisonné. Thomson a créé un effet de vitrail dans son tableau *Le Pin* (Musée des beaux-arts du Canada, Ottawa), bien que cet effet évoque davantage les vitraux de Louis Comfort Tiffany que ceux de l'art médiéval. Sa véritable contribution au postimpressionnisme réside dans son utilisation du paysage nordique et son affection pour la structure du sol. Les membres du Groupe des Sept devaient se rappeler plus tard avoir trouvé dans l'œuvre du Thomson de 1912, les premières traces du motif qui allait dominer leur travail.

1. Interview d'A.Y. Jackson par l'auteure, 4 mars 1971. Joan Murray, Tom Thomson Papers.

2. Interview de Jackson.

3. Lettre d'A.Y. Jackson, 13 octobre 1914, et lettre de F.H. Varley, adressées l'une et l'autre au D[r] J.M. MacCallum, octobre 1914, Correspondance MacCallum, Archives du Musée des beaux-arts du Canada.

Appendix: Recollections

Despite the occasionally sexist tone common to the times, John Lyman's tribute to Henri Matisse draws a lively picture of Matisse's atelier.

John Lyman, "Adieu, Matisse"*

Henri Matisse is dead. What a contradiction in terms!

For the last fourteen miraculous years he had defied mortality. It had always seemed paradoxical that the work of this sober, reflective man, with the grave mien of a doctor, looked as though it had been dashed off in a moment of gay exuberance but since, following an operation at the age of 72, he had become partially incapacitated, unable to leave his bed for more than half a day, his art had grown incredibly in youthfulness and vitality.

My first acquaintance with Matisse's painting was when, in the spring of 1909, I saw his *Fontainebleau Forest* in the Salon des Indépendents. Its summary intensity haunted my dreams. In the fall, Matthew Smith and I (we had become friends a year earlier at Étaples) resolved to attend the "Académie Matisse." Nothing could have been less academic than this nest of heretical fledglings, lodged in a disused convent under the trees of an ancient garden.

That was the time when everybody said of a picture by Matisse: "My six-year-old child could do better than that." Today it is said in certain avant-garde circles that his painting is too facile. There is no real difference between the two statements except that the earlier one was excusable because it was evoked by naive surprise at a spontaneity that had not been seen since at least the Middle Ages.

Facile, his painting? Blind or dogmatic he who can say so. If Matisse rarely repainted, he began his picture again on a fresh canvas five, ten, fifteen times, until the moment of final decanting was reached. It was the same with his drawings: trial sheet after sheet fluttered to the floor until, with final concentration, he condensed into the subtle modulation of a line an incredible wealth of content.

He was quick to censure the superficial device, the merely decorative abbreviation, the lack of "density" as he always called it. That was the burden of his teaching. Students who came to him to learn modern tricks got no encouragement. "Learn to walk on the ground before you try the tight-rope" was his constant reminder.

Continental art teachers seldom criticize oftener than once a week; Matisse visited us only once a fortnight and then his criticism usually took the form of a long chat about fundamental principles and qualities. We were about fifteen in the school. The late Edward Bruce was *massier*. Besides Matthew Smith there was Per Krog who became a leading painter in his native Norway, Hans Purrmann, a number of other Germans and Scandinavians, and some Austrian women whose most memorable aesthetic gift was their own blond beauty.**

Once Matisse invited us to his house at Issy-les-Moulineaux, the house with the large studio where, besides the two versions of *La Desserte*, the *Red Interior* and dozens of other well-known pictures, he painted *The Dance*, which was there at the time.

*Reprinted from *Canadian Art* 12, 2 (Winter 1955), pp. 44–46.

**In the photograph of the Académie Matisse (p. 13), Hans Purrmann is eighth from the left; César the *massier* is directly behind Lyman and in the background.

Later I came to know the model with the glowing skin (we nicknamed her "Italian sunset") whom Matisse had taken south with him in the summer and who, posing among green pines against the Mediterranean blue, had suggested the colour of *The Dance*.

That was the last year of the "Académie Matisse." I returned home and married. It was in the year when I held my first exhibition that so scandalized Montreal, 1913, that the famous Armory Exhibition introduced Matisse to America, to the delight of us youngsters and the annoyance of critics and curators who then were not prone to recognize new genius. (Today, to live down that reputation, they recognize genius that has not yet appeared.)

It was not until after the war that I saw Matisse again. On a visit to Nice, we found him on the balcony of the hotel room on the Promenade des Anglais (where he did most of his work between 1917 and 1920) painting *La Fête des Fleurs à Nice*. In an unusually playful mood, he was swinging his brush in time with the band music. The looping brushwork did not produce a very good picture; he was just having fun. When we returned to the Côte d'Azur a couple of years later, he had moved to that spacious, high-ceilinged apartment with the great windows overlooking Les Ponchettes and the bay. We went there to pay our respects, and he showed us all his recent work, canvas after canvas. Words were soon obliterated from my mind by the sight of so much lyric splendour. Matisse must have understood for he did not seem in the least put out by my failure to exclaim. In the next few years we saw him only infrequently when, stopping over in Paris, he appeared at a dress rehearsal or a concert.

He was always a great believer in regular work, and at that time his strict daily routine was: 8 to 9 a.m., violin; 9 to 12, model for painting; after lunch, a short stroll, then model again for drawing; a light supper, a stroll and bed, with a book (perhaps a classic or Mallarmé or Valéry) by his bed-side in case he woke up in the night. The only variation was on Sunday afternoon, when he went to play chamber music with friends.

But few things could distract him from his work. His hand could not remain "silent" for long: soon his pencil was at play. Nature was his constant source and reference, no matter how much its particular aspects were modified to suit his general conception. While he worked he had the feeling that he was copying nature and that every deviation was for the purpose of expressing it more completely.

There is no phase of his work that does not bear witness to this intention. Even in his latest painting, where his synthesis approaches abstraction, every form and colour chord has the ring of truth, awakening prolonged echoes of recognition. Untouched by the doubts and withdrawals that afflict the age, his art is not a refusal but an affirmation of life.

As Ian M. Thom points out, Carr learned a great deal from Phelan Gibb, a British expatriate living in Paris who was friendly with Matisse.

Emily Carr Writing About Her Teacher, Henry (Harry) Phelan Gibb*

About Gibb's painting: "I was puzzled, the scene was more than what was before us. It was not a copy of the woods & fields, it was a realization of them. The colors were not matched, they mixed with air. You went through space to meet reality. Space was the saliva that made your objects swallowable. Harry Gibb had worked in Spain. He had fed on color and atmosphere and acquired the taste."

About Crécy-en-Brie: "That session with Gibb down in Crécy-en-Brie woke me."

*Emily Carr, Manuscript for *Growing Pains*, Provincial Archives and Records Service, Victoria, quoted in Ian M. Thom, *Emily Carr in France* (Vancouver: Vancouver Art Gallery, 1991), pp. 16–17. Carr's writings have been edited for spelling; her words are unchanged.

Anne Savage Speaking About William Brymner and Paul Cézanne*

"Brymner was way ahead of his time ... they had a memorial show of Brymners, and there were some beautiful things in the meadows, they might have been Renoirs or Pissarros, they were just beautiful.... Beautiful greens and pinks.... That was the thing that he brought to us, and we got it just drop by drop ... we couldn't get reproductions of these.... We'd search them out in magazines and postcards and prints and the excitement when you found something of [word missing from transcript] or something would come out in one of the magazines, and I remember in ... 1913, the Armory show was on.... And we knew there was a man called Cézanne. I was so interested in him because his birth date was the same as my father's. He was born in, in 18— wait a minute, he died in 19— no he was born in 1840, that's right, and he died in 1906. My father was born in 1840. So I thought, well, isn't that interesting – and you see, that sort of made me feel much closer to Cézanne. I realized he wasn't just a way off, away, miles and miles away, he was really quite close to us in our context. There was such a human being, just about our same vintage, working in France.... Brymner had a dry wit.... He had the quality of being able to let other people do the talking and when they had finished he would sum the whole thing up with just one simple remark. He was very delightful."

*Anne Savage in conversation with Arthur Calvin, "Anne Savage, Teacher," Master's thesis, Sir George Williams University, Montreal, 1967, unpublished; paginated typescript of interview, Arthur Calvin with Anne Savage, p. 23. Anne Savage Papers, Concordia University Archives, Montreal.

Appendice: Souvenirs et témoignages

En dépit de son ton sexiste, typique de l'époque, l'hommage de John Lyman à Henri Matisse offre une description vivante de l'atelier de Matisse.

« Adieu, Matisse »*, de John Lyman

Henri Matisse est mort. Quelle contradiction dans les termes!

Pendant les quatorze dernières années de sa vie, années miraculeuses, il a défié la mort. Il a toujours semblé paradoxal que l'œuvre de cet homme sérieux et pensif, à la mine grave d'un médecin, donne l'impression d'avoir été exécutée précipitamment, dans un moment de gaieté exubérante. Pourtant, bien qu'une opération à l'âge de 72 ans l'ait laissé partiellement invalide, incapable de quitter son lit pour plus d'une demi-journée, son art, incroyablement, ne cessait de se faire plus jeune et plus vital.

Mon premier contact avec la peinture de Matisse a eu lieu au printemps de 1909, lorsque j'ai vu *La forêt de Fontainebleau* au Salon des Indépendants. Son intensité condensée hantait mes rêves. À l'automne, Matthew Smith et moi-même (nous nous étions liés plus tôt à Étaples) avons résolu de nous inscrire à l'« Académie Matisse ». Rien n'aurait pu être moins académique que ce nid d'oiselets hérétiques, placés dans un couvent désaffecté sous les arbres d'un ancien jardin.

C'était l'époque où chacun s'exclamait à propos d'un tableau de Matisse : « Mon gosse de six ans aurait pu faire mieux que ça ». Aujourd'hui dans certains cercles d'avant-garde, cette peinture est jugée trop facile. Il n'y a pas de différence entre ces deux opinions sauf que la première est excusable, car elle représente la surprise naïve face à une spontanéité qui ne s'était pas vue depuis au moins le Moyen-Âge.

Facile, cette peinture? Il faut être aveugle ou dogmatique pour le proclamer. Si Matisse retouchait rarement un tableau, il recommençait sans cesse sa peinture sur un nouveau canevas, cinq, dix, quinze fois, jusqu'à l'atteinte du décantement final. La même chose se produisait pour ses dessins : les pages tourbillonnaient vers le sol l'une après l'autre jusqu'à ce que, dans un moment de concentration finale, il ait condensé dans le subtil modelé d'une ligne un contenu d'une richesse incroyable.

Il était prompt à supprimer le superficiel, l'abréviation purement décorative, le manque de « densité » comme il disait. C'était là la difficulté de son enseignement. Les étudiants venus vers lui pour apprendre des trucs modernes ne recevaient aucun encouragement. « Apprenez à marcher sur le sol avant d'essayer la corde raide », rappelait-il constamment.

Les professeurs d'art européens faisaient rarement leurs critiques plus d'une fois par semaine; Matisse, lui, nous rendait visite seulement une fois tous les quinze jours et sa critique prenait alors la forme d'un long discours sur les qualités et les principes fondamentaux de l'art. Nous étions à peu près quinze dans l'école. Le défunt Edward Bruce était *massier*. Outre Matthew Smith, il y avait Per Krog (devenu un peintre de premier plan dans sa Norvège natale), Hans Purmann, un certain nombre d'autres allemands et scandinaves, et quelques femmes autrichiennes plus mémorables pour leur beauté blonde que pour leur don esthétique.**

*Reproduit de *Canadian Art* 12, 2 (hiver 1955), p. 44–46

** Dans la photographie montrant l'Académie Matisse (p. 13), Hans Purrmann est le huitième à partir de la gauche; au fond, juste derrière John Lyman, on voit César, *massier* (comme l'appelait Matisse).

Un jour, Matisse nous a invités à sa maison à Issy-les-Moulineaux, la maison au grand atelier où, en plus des deux versions de *La Desserte*, d'*Intérieur rouge* et de douzaines d'autres tableaux bien connus, il a peint *La Danse*, qui se trouvait là à l'époque. J'ai connu plus tard la personne à la peau rougeoyante qui lui a servi de modèle (nous l'avions baptisée son « coucher de soleil italien »); Matisse l'avait emmenée avec lui dans le Midi, et elle lui avait inspiré la couleur de *La Danse* en posant parmi les pins verts se détachant sur la bleue Méditerranée.

C'était la dernière année de l' « Académie Matisse ». Je suis revenu chez moi et me suis marié. C'était l'année où j'ai eu ma première exposition, qui a tant scandalisé Montréal en 1913, la même année que celle du célèbre Armory Show qui a révélé Matisse à l'Amérique, pour notre plus grand plaisir à nous les jeunes et pour l'agacement des critiques et des conservateurs qui n'ont pas su reconnaître le nouveau génie. (Aujourd'hui, pour faire oublier leur manque de discernement à cette occasion, ils reconnaissent le génie qui ne s'est pas encore manifesté.)

J'ai revu Matisse après la guerre seulement. Lors d'une visite à Nice, nous l'avons trouvé sur le balcon d'une chambre d'hôtel donnant sur la Promenade des Anglais où il a peint presque toutes ses œuvres entre 1917 et 1920, et qu'on reconnaît dans *La Fête des Fleurs à Nice*. D'humeur exceptionnellement enjouée, il battait de son pinceau la mesure d'une fanfare. La brosse ainsi manipulée n'a pas donné lieu à un très bon tableau; Matisse s'amusait tout simplement. À notre retour sur la côte d'Azur deux ans plus tard, il avait déménagé dans un appartement spacieux aux hauts plafonds, avec de grandes fenêtres s'ouvrant sur Les Ponchettes et la baie. Nous sommes allés lui rendre visite, et il nous a montré tous ses récents tableaux, toile après toile. La vue d'une telle splendeur lyrique m'a bientôt coupé la parole. Matisse a dû comprendre car il ne semblait pas le moins du monde offusqué par mon silence. Dans les années qui suivirent, nous l'avons vu à l'occasion seulement lorsque, de passage à Paris, il se trouvait à une répétition ou un concert.

Il a toujours cru au travail régulier, et à cette époque sa stricte routine quotidienne se déroulait comme suit : de 8 h à 9 h, violon; de 9 h à midi, peinture d'après un modèle; après le déjeuner, petite promenade, puis dessin, de nouveau d'après un modèle; léger souper, promenade et coucher, un livre sur sa table de chevet (un classique peut-être, ou Mallarmé ou Valéry) au cas où il s'éveille pendant la nuit. La seule dérogation à ce régime avait lieu le dimanche après-midi; il allait alors jouer de la musique de chambre avec des amis.

Peu de choses pouvaient le distraire de son travail. Sa main ne pouvait demeurer longtemps « silencieuse » : vite, il se mettait à jouer avec son crayon. La nature était sa source constante de référence, peu importe les modifications qu'il apportait à certains de ses aspects pour réaliser sa conception générale. Au travail, il avait le sentiment de copier la nature : les déviations qu'il se permettait servaient seulement à en faire une rendition plus juste.

Il n'est pas dans son œuvre une seule phase qui ne témoigne de cette intention. Même dans son dernier tableau, où la synthèse se rapproche de l'abstraction, chaque accord de formes ou de couleurs sonne vrai, et nous le reconnaissons par l'écho prolongé de cette musique en nous. Imperméable aux doutes et aux retraits qui affligent la vieillesse, son art n'est pas un refus, mais une affirmation de la vie.

Comme le note Ian M. Thom, Carr a beaucoup appris de Gibb, expatrié britannique vivant à Paris et ami de Matisse.

Emily Carr écrivant à propos de son professeur, Henry (Harry) Phelan Gibb*

À propos de la peinture de Gibb : « J'étais intriguée, la scène était plus que ce qu'il y avait devant nous. Ce n'était pas une copie exacte des bois et des champs, mais une réalisation de ces éléments. Les couleurs n'étaient pas assorties, elles se mêlaient à l'air. On passait par l'espace pour rencontrer le réel. L'espace était la salive qui permettait d'avaler les objets. Harry Gibb avait travaillé en Espagne. Il s'était nourri de sa couleur et de son ambiance, et en avait pris le goût. »

À propos de Crécy-en-Brie : « Cette session avec Gibb à Crécy-en-Brie m'a éveillée. »

*Emily Carr, manuscrit de *Growing Pains*, Provincial Archives and Records Service, Victoria, cité par Ian M. Thom dans *Emily Carr in France* (catalogue d'exposition) (Vancouver : Vancouver Art Gallery, 1991), p. 16–17. L'épellation a été corrigée dans les écrits de Carr, mais sans altérer les propos du peintre.

Anne Savage dans une conversation sur William Brymner et Paul Cézanne*

« … Brymner était de beaucoup en avance sur son temps… en hommage à sa mémoire, on a monté une exposition de ses œuvres, et il y avait de belles choses dans ses prés, ç'aurait pu être des Renoirs ou des Pissarros, c'était tout simplement beau… De beaux verts et roses… C'était ça la chose qu'il nous avait apportée, et que nous avons reçue à petites gouttes… on ne pouvait pas se procurer de reproductions de ces choses. Nous les cherchions dans des revues et des cartes postales et des imprimés, et l'excitation quand on trouvait quelque chose de [un mot manque dans le manuscrit], ou quand quelque chose paraissait dans une revue, je me souviens en… 1913, l'Armory Show avait lieu… Et nous savions qu'il y avait un homme qui s'appelait Cézanne. J'étais particulièrement intéressée à lui car sa date d'anniversaire était la même que celle de mon père. Il est né en, en 18 – attendez une seconde, il est mort en 19 – non, il est né en 1840, c'est cela, et il est mort en 1906. Mon père est né en 1840. Alors, je pensais, eh bien, n'est-ce pas que c'est intéressant – et vous voyez, cela m'a fait me sentir beaucoup plus près de Cézanne. Je me suis rendu compte qu'il n'était pas loin de nous, à des milles et des milles, il était en fait vraiment près de nous, il faisait partie de notre contexte. Il existait un être humain comme lui, d'à peu près la même époque que nous, qui travaillait en France… Brymner avait l'esprit caustique… Il savait laisser les autres parler et quand ils avaient fini il résumait leurs palabres en une seule remarque toute simple. Il était merveilleux. »

*Anne Savage en conversation avec Arthur Calvin, « Anne Savage, Teacher », thèse de maîtrise, Université Sir George Williams, Montréal, 1967, inédite; pagination de l'entrevue dactylographiée, Arthur Calvin et Anne Savage, p. 23. Documents Anne Savage, Archives de l'Université Concordia, Montréal.

Catalogue of the Exhibition / Les œuvres de l'exposition

Cecil Buller, 1886–1973

1. *Market, Concarneau*, c. 1915 / *Marché à Concarneau*, v. 1915
Oil on canvas / Huile sur toile, 74.0 x 91.5 cm
National Gallery of Canada / Musée des beaux-arts du Canada, Ottawa
Gift of Sean B. Murphy, Montreal, 1997 / Don de Sean B. Murphy, Montréal, 1997

Franklin Carmichael, 1890–1945

2. *Winter Hillside / Colline en hiver*, 1918 (?)
Oil on canvas / Huile sur toile, 40.7 x 45.6 cm
McMichael Canadian Art Collection / Collection McMichael d'art canadien, Kleinburg
Gift of Mr. and Mrs. R.G. Mastin / Don de M. et Mme R.G. Mastin

3. *Untitled*, c. 1920 / *Sans titre*, v. 1920
Oil on board / Huile sur panneau, 25.5 x 30.6 cm
The Robert McLaughlin Gallery, Oshawa
Gift of John and Hélène Mastin / Don de John et Hélène Mastin, 1998

4. *The Glade / La Clairière*, 1922
Oil on canvas / Huile sur toile, 63 x 75.5 cm
University College Art Collection, University of Toronto, Toronto

Emily Carr, 1871–1945

5. *Breton Farm Yard*, 1912 (?) / *Cour de ferme bretonne*, 1912 (?)
Oil on laminated pulp board / Huile sur toile cartonnée, 32.3 x 40.8 cm
McMichael Canadian Art Collection / Collection McMichael d'art canadien, Kleinburg
Gift of F. Joy Peinhof-Wright / Don de F. Joy Peinhof-Wright

6. *Yan, Q.C.I.*, 1912
Oil on canvas / Huile sur toile, 98.8 x 152.5 cm
Art Gallery of Hamilton, Hamilton
Gift of Roy G. Cole / Don de Roy G. Cole, 1992

7. *Trees / Arbres*, 1919
Oil on burlap / Huile sur toile de jute, 45.8 x 61.0 cm
Private Collection / Collection privée, Winnipeg

Emily Coonan, 1885–1917

8. *Girl with a Rose / Jeune fille à la rose*, 1913
Oil on canvas / Huile sur toile, 76.6 x 53.5 cm
National Gallery of Canada / Musée des beaux-arts du Canada, Ottawa
Purchased / Acquise en 1997

9. *Girl in Green*, c. 1913 / *Jeune fille en vert*, v. 1913
Oil on canvas / Huile sur toile, 66.4 x 49.0 cm
Art Gallery of Hamilton, Hamilton
Gift of A.Y. Jackson, C.M.G., R.C.A. / Don de A.Y. Jackson, 1956

Lawren (Stewart) Harris, 1885–1970

10. *Autumn [Kempenfelt Bay, Lake Simcoe]*, c. 1916–1917 / *Automne [Baie Kempenfelt, Lac Simcoe]*, v. 1916–1917

Oil on canvas / Huile sur toile, 97.5 x 110.0 cm

University College Art Collection, University of Toronto, Toronto

11. *Snow / La Neige*, 1917 (?)

Oil on canvas / Huile sur toile, 71.0 x 110.1 cm

McMichael Canadian Art Collection / Collection McMichael d'art canadien, Kleinburg

Gift of Mr. and Mrs. Keith MacIver / Don de M. et Mme Keith MacIver

12. *Hubert, Above Montreal Falls*, c. 1919 / *Hubert, Au-dessus des chutes de Montréal*, v. 1919

Oil on board / Huile sur panneau, 34.9 x 26.7 cm

Private Collection / Collection privée, Toronto

Adrien Hébert, 1890–1967

13. *"Enclos," Belair Island / L'Enclos, Île Bélair*, 1921

Oil on canvas / Huile sur toile, 30.5 x 40.6 cm

National Gallery of Canada / Musée des beaux-arts du Canada, Ottawa

Purchased / Acquise en 1978

Randolph S. Hewton, 1888–1960

14. *Afternoon, Camaret*, c. 1913 / *Après-Midi, Camaret*, v. 1913

Oil on canvas / Huile sur toile, 71.5 x 59.2 cm

McMichael Canadian Art Collection / Collection McMichael d'art canadien, Kleinburg

Gift of Mr. and Mrs. H.J. Campbell / Don de M. et Mme H.J. Campbell

15. *Birches*, c. 1921 / *Bouleaux*, v. 1921

Oil on canvas / Huile sur toile, 63.5 x 58.4 cm

Private Collection / Collection privée, Whitby

Edwin (Headley) Holgate, 1892–1977

16. *Festival of Blue Nets / Fête des filets bleus, Concarneau*, 1921

Oil on canvas / Huile sur toile, 60.3 x 73.4 cm

Art Gallery of Hamilton, Hamilton

Gift of *The Hamilton Spectator* / Don de *The Hamilton Spectator*, 1972

Alexander Young (A.Y.) Jackson, 1882–1974

17. *Springtime in Picardy / Printemps en Picardie*, 1919

Oil on canvas / Huile sur toile, 65.1 x 77.5 cm

Collection, Art Gallery of Ontario, Toronto / Collection, Musée des beaux-arts de l'Ontario, Toronto

Gift from the Albert H. Robson Memorial Subscription Fund, 1940 / Don de l'Albert H. Robson Memorial Subscription Fund, 1940

Arthur Lismer, 1885–1969

18. *Winter / Hiver*, 1920

Oil on linen / Huile sur toile de lin, 50.9 x 61.7 cm

Edmonton Art Gallery Collection, Edmonton

Gift of Ernest E. Poole Foundation / Don de la Fondation Ernest E. Poole

John Lyman, 1886–1967

19. *Café, rue Royal, Paris*, 1909 (?)

Oil on wood / Huile sur bois, 11.0 x 18.0 cm

Musée du Québec, Ville de Québec

20. *Landscape, Bermuda*, c. 1914 / *Paysage, Bermudes*, v. 1914
Oil on canvas / Huile sur toile, 55.4 x 45.9 cm
National Gallery of Canada / Musée des beaux-arts du Canada, Ottawa
Purchased / Acquise en 1944

21. *Portrait of Corinne / Portrait de Corinne*, 1919
Oil on canvas / Huile sur toile, 84.0 x 61.5 cm
Musée du Québec, Ville de Québec

James Edward Hervey (J.E.H.) MacDonald, 1873–1932

22. *Garden Flowers*, c. 1915 / *Fleurs du jardin*, v. 1915
Oil on board / Huile sur panneau, 20.0 x 14.6 cm
Private Collection / Collection privée, Toronto

23. *Evening, Mongoose Lake / Soir, Lac Mongoose*, 1920
Oil on card / Huile sur carton, 21.6 x 26.7 cm
Museum London, Art Fund, 1948, London

24. *Mist Fantasy, Northland / Fantaisie brumeuse, Northland*, 1922
Oil on canvas / Huile sur toile, 53.7 x 66.7 cm
Art Gallery of Ontario / Musée des beaux-arts de l'Ontario, Toronto
Gift of Mrs. S.J. Williams, Toronto, in memory of Elinor Williams /
Don de M^me^ S.J. Williams, en mémoire d'Elinor Williams, 1927

Florence H. McGillivray, 1864–1938

25. *Contentment / Contentement*, 1913
Oil on cardboard / Huile sur carton, 41.0 x 32.7 cm
Art Gallery of Ontario / Musée des beaux-arts de l'Ontario, Toronto
Gift of Miss F.H. McGillivray / Don de M^lle^ F.H. McGillivray, 1937

26. *Canal, Venice / Canal, Venise*, 1917
Oil on board / Huile sur panneau, 33.0 x 40.6 cm
Private Collection / Collection privée, Whitby

27. *Venice / Venise*, 1918 (?)
Oil on canvas / Huile sur toile, 77.5 x 129.0 cm
Trafalgar Castle School, Whitby

(Edward) Middleton Manigault, 1887–1922

28. *Procession*, 1911
Oil on canvas / Huile sur toile, 50.8 x 60.96 cm
Columbus Museum of Art, Columbus, Ohio
Gift of Ferdinand Howald / Don de Ferdinand Howald
(Oshawa only / seulement à Oshawa)

29. *Mountainous Landscape (or Wide Valley) / Paysage montagnard (ou Grande vallée)*, 1913
Oil on canvas / Huile sur toile, 45.8 x 84.1 cm
Arnot Art Museum, Elmira, New York
Gift of Charles C. Rumsey / Don de Charles C. Rumsey, 1960

(Henrietta) Mabel May, 1884–1971

30. *Indian Woman – Oka / Femme indienne – Oka*, 1917
Oil on canvas / Huile sur toile, 66.4 x 53.9 cm
Art Gallery of Hamilton, Hamilton
Bequest of Josephine M. Magee / Legs Josephine M. Magee, 1958

David Milne, 1881–1953

31. *Blue Interior*, c. 1913 / *Intérieur bleu*, v. 1913
Oil on canvas / Huile sur toile, 51.1 x 46.0 cm
McMichael Canadian Art Collection / Collection McMichael d'art canadien, Kleinburg
Purchased / Acquise, 1972

32. *Tree and Grey Rocks / Arbres et rochers gris*, 1914
Oil on canvas / Huile sur toile, 55.9 x 50.8 cm
Private Collection / Collection privée, Toronto

33. *Black / Noir*, 1914
Oil on canvas / Huile sur toile, 51.9 x 62.1 cm
McMichael Canadian Art Collection / Collection McMichael d'art canadien, Kleinburg
Gift of the Founders, Robert and Signe McMichael / Don à la collection de la part des fondateurs, Robert et Signe McMichael

34. *Icebox with Kitchen Shelves / Glacière avec étagères de cuisine*, 1919
Watercolour on paper / Aquarelle sur papier, 44.7 x 55.1 cm
Museum London, London
Bequest of Mrs. Frances Barwick / Legs M^me Frances Barwick, Ottawa, 1985

James Wilson Morrice, 1865–1924

35. *North African Town*, c. 1912–1913 / *Ville d'Afrique du Nord*, v. 1912–1913
Oil and graphite on panel / Huile et fusain sur panneau, 9.9 x 15.7 cm
The Robert McLaughlin Gallery, Oshawa
Gift of the estate of Eleanor and David R. Morrice / Don de la succession d'Eleanor et David R. Morrice, 1979

36. *View of a North African Town*, c. 1912–1913 / *Vue d'une ville d'Afrique du Nord*, v. 1912–1913
Oil on panel / Huile sur panneau, 12.2 x 15.0 cm
Art Gallery of Hamilton, Hamilton
Bequest of David R. Morrice / Legs David R. Morrice, 1978

37. *Afternoon, Tunis*, c. 1914 / *L'après-midi à Tunis*, v. 1914
Oil on canvas / Huile sur toile, 54.3 x 64.7 cm
Montreal Museum of Fine Arts / Musée des beaux-arts de Montréal, Montréal
Purchase / Acquisition, John W. Tempest Fund

38. *Village Street, West Indies*, c. 1915–1919 / *Rue d'un village aux Antilles*, v. 1915–1919
Oil on canvas / Huile sur toile, 60.2 x 82.0 cm
Montreal Museum of Fine Arts / Musée des beaux-arts de Montréal, Montréal
Purchase / Acquisition, William Gilman Cheney Fund

39. *Quebec Farmhouse*, c. 1921 / *Maison de ferme québécoise*, v. 1921
Oil on canvas / Huile sur toile, 81.2 x 60.3 cm
Montreal Museum of Fine Arts / Musée des beaux-arts de Montréal, Montréal
Bequest of William J. Morrice / Legs William J. Morrice

Albert Henry (A.H.) Robinson

40. *Noontime, Longue Pointe Village / Midi, village de Longue Pointe*, 1919
Oil on canvas / Huile sur toile, 76.7 x 101.8 cm
Musée du Québec, Ville de Québec

Anne Savage, 1896–1971

41. *Untitled (Canal)*, c. 1915–1918 / *Sans titre (Canal)*, v. 1915–1918
Oil on wood / Huile sur bois, 15.8 x 22.1 cm
National Gallery of Canada / Musée des beaux-arts du Canada, Ottawa
Gift of John B. Claxton, Q.C., Anne McDougall, Galt MacDermot, Mary-Drummond, and Helen Leslie, 1997 / Don de John B. Claxton, c.r., Anne McDougall, Galt MacDermot, Mary Drummond et Helen Leslie, 1997

42. *Portrait of William Brymner / Portrait de William Brymner*, 1919
Oil on board / Huile sur carton, 22.8 x 17.8 cm
Art Gallery of Hamilton, Hamilton
Gift of the artist / Don de l'artiste, 1959

Thomas John (Tom) Thomson, 1877–1917

43. *Phantom Tent*, c. 1915 / *Tente fantôme*, v. 1915
Oil on panel / Huile sur panneau, 21.2 x 26.7 cm
McMichael Canadian Art Collection / Collection McMichael d'art canadien, Kleinburg
Gift of Mr. R.A. Laidlaw / Don de M. R.A. Laidlaw

44. *Autumn Trees, Algonquin Park*, c. 1915–1916 / *Arbres en automne, Parc Algonquin*, v. 1915–1916
Oil on board / Huile sur carton, 26.7 x 21.6 cm
Private Collection / Collection privée, Toronto

45. *Autumn Birches*, c. 1916 / *Bouleaux en automne*, v. 1916
Oil on panel / Huile sur panneau, 21.6 x 26.7 cm
McMichael Canadian Art Collection / Collection McMichael d'art canadien, Kleinburg
Gift of Mrs. H.P. de Pencier / Don de M^{me} H.P. de Pencier

46 (recto and verso / recto et verso). *Nocturne*, c. 1916 / *Nocturne*, v. 1916
Oil on board / Huile sur carton, 22.0 x 27.1 cm
Private Collection / Collection privée, Trenton

47. *The Drive*, c. 1916 / *La Drave*, v. 1916
Oil on canvas / Huile sur toile, 132.0 x 150.0 cm
Ontario Agricultural College purchase with funds raised by students, faculty and staff / Acquisition de l'Ontario Agricultural College grâce à une levée de fonds réalisée par les étudiants, la faculté et le personnel, 1926
University of Guelph Collection / Collection de l'Université de Guelph
MacDonald Stewart Art Centre, Guelph
(Oshawa and Montreal only / Seulement à Oshawa et à Montréal)

Further Reading / Ouvrages recommandés

General / Lectures d'intérêt général

The Advent of Modernism: Post-Impressionism and North American Art, 1900–1918 (Atlanta: High Museum of Art, 1986).

Brettell, Richard R. *Modern Art 1851–1929* (Oxford: Oxford University Press, 1999).

Denvir, Bernard. *Post-Impressionism* (London: Thames and Hudson, 1992).

Jasen, Patricia. *Wild Things: Nature, Culture, and Tourism in Ontario, 1790–1914* (Toronto: University of Toronto Press, 1995).

Lowrey, Carol, et al. *Visions of Light and Air: Canadian Impressionism, 1885–1920* (New York: Americas Society Art Gallery, 1995). [This catalogue has an excellent and wide-ranging bibliography. / Ce catalogue offre une vaste et excellente bibliographie.]

Mastin, Catharine. *Canadian Artists in Paris and the French Influence* (Calgary: Glenbow Museum, 2000).

O'Brian, John. *Ruthless Hedonism: The American Reception of Matisse* (Chicago & London: University of Chicago Press, 1999).

Ostiguy, Jean-René. *Modernism in Quebec Art, 1916-1946* (Ottawa: National Gallery of Art, 1982).

———. *Les esthétiques modernes au Québec de 1916 à 1946* (Ottawa: Galerie nationale du Canada [aujourd'hui: Musée des beaux-arts du Canada], 1982).

Post-Impressionism: Cross-Currents in European and American Painting, 1880–1906 (Washington: National Gallery of Art, 1980).

Rewald, John. *Cézanne and America: Dealers, Collectors, Artists and Critics, 1891–1921* (Princeton: Princeton University Press, 1989).

Trépanier, Esther. *Peinture et Modernité au Québec, 1919-1939* (Québec: Éditions Nota bene, 1998).

The Armory Show and Canadian Art / L'Armory Show et l'art canadien

Dwight, Edward. "The Armory Show – New York 1913," *Canadian Art* 84 (March–April 1963 / mars–avril 1963), pp. 118–119.

Beaver Hall Group / Le Groupe de Beaver Hall

Meadowcroft, Barbara. *Painting Friends: The Beaver Hall Women Painters* (Montreal: Véhicule Press, 1999).

Cecil Buller

Ainslie, Patricia. *Cecil Buller: Modernist Printmaker* (Calgary: Glenbow Museum, 1989).

Mari et Femme : L'œuvre gravé de John J.A. Murphy et Cecil Buller (Québec: Musée du Québec, 1997).

Canadian Art Club

Lamb, Robert J. *The Canadian Art Club 1907–1915* (Edmonton: Edmonton Art Gallery, 1988).

Franklin Carmichael

Bice, Megan. *Light & Shadow: The Work of Franklin Carmichael* (Kleinburg: McMichael Canadian Art Collection, 1990).

Emily Carr

Carr, Emily. *Growing Pains* (Toronto: Oxford, 1946).

Moray, Greta. *Unsettling Encounters: The Indian Pictures of Emily Carr* (forthcoming / à paraître).

Shadbolt, Doris. *Emily Carr* (Vancouver/Toronto: Douglas & McIntyre, 1990).

Steward, Jay, and Peter Macnair. *To the Totem Forests: Emily Carr and Contemporaries Interpret Coastal Villages* (Victoria: Art Gallery of Greater Victoria, 1999).

Thom, Ian M. *Emily Carr in France* (Vancouver: Vancouver Art Gallery, 1991).

Emily Coonan

Emily Coonan (1885–1971) (Montreal: Concordia Art Gallery, 1987). (Essays by Karen Antaki and Sandra Paikowsky / Avec des contributions de Karen Antaki et Sandra Paikowsky.)

First World War and Its Impact on Artists / La Première Guerre mondiale et son influence sur les artistes

Oliver, Dean F., and Laura Brandon. *Canvas of War: Painting the Canadian Experience, 1914-1945* (Vancouver: Douglas & McIntyre, 2000).

———. *Tableaux de guerre : peindre l'expérience canadienne de 1914 à 1945* (Outremont, Québec : Éditions du Trécarré, 2000).

Group of Seven / Le Groupe des Sept

Hill, Charles C. *The Group of Seven: Art for a Nation* (Ottawa: National Gallery of Canada; Toronto: McClelland & Stewart, 1995).

———. *Le Groupe des Sept : l'émergence d'un art national* (Ottawa : Musée des beaux-arts du Canada, 1995).

Lawren Harris

Adamson, Jeremy. *Lawren S. Harris: Urban Scenes and Wilderness Landscapes, 1906–1930* (Toronto: Art Gallery of Ontario, 1978).

Foss, Brian. "'Synchronism' in Canada: Lawren Harris, Decorative Landscape, and Willard Huntington Wright, 1916–1917," *Journal of Canadian Art History* 20, 1 & 2 (1999), pp. 68-88.

Larisey, Peter. *Light for a Cold Land: Lawren Harris's Work and Life – An Interpretation* (Toronto: Dundurn, 1993).

Prakash, Ash. "Lawren Stewart Harris (1885–1970)," *Magazin Art* 12, 2 (Spring / Printemps 2000), pp. 84–88, 115–119.

Adrien Hébert

L'Allier, Pierre (dir.). *Adrien Hébert* (Québec : Musée du Québec, 1993).

Ostiguy, Jean-René. *Adrien Hébert, premier interprète de la modernité québécoise* (Saint-Laurent : Éditions du Trécarré, 1986).

———. *Adrien Hébert: Thirty Years of His Art, 1923-1953* (Ottawa: National Gallery of Canada, 1971).

———. *Adrien Hébert, trente ans de son œuvre 1923–1953* (Ottawa : Galerie nationale du Canada, 1971).

———. "Le Modernisme au Québec en 1910 et en 1930," *Vie des Arts* 27, 107 (Spring / Printemps 1982), pp. 42–45.

———. "Les Influences cézanniennes chez Adrien Hébert," *Annual Bulletin* 7, National Gallery of Canada, 1982–1983 (1985), pp. 31–45.

———. *Modernism in Quebec Art, 1916 to 1946* (Ottawa: National Gallery of Canada, 1982).

Edwin Holgate

Prakash, Ash. "Edwin Headley Holgate (1892–1977): Master of Sculptured Painting," *Magazin Art* 12, 2 (Winter / Hiver 1999–2000), pp. 69–72, 92–96.

Reid, Dennis. *Edwin H. Holgate* (Ottawa : National Gallery of Canada, 1976).

———. *Edwin H. Holgate* (Ottawa : Galerie nationale du Canada, 1976).

Alexander Young (A.Y.) Jackson

Jackson, A.Y. *A Painter's Country: The Autobiography of A.Y. Jackson* (Toronto: Clarke, Irwin & Co., 1976).

Arthur Lismer

Harris, Lawren. *Arthur Lismer: Paintings, 1913–1949* (Toronto: Art Gallery of Toronto, 1950).

John Lyman

Dompierre, Louise. *John Lyman: 1886–1967* (Kingston: Agnes Etherington Art Centre, Queen's University, 1986).

Varley, Christopher. *The Contemporary Arts Society, Montréal, 1939–1948* (Edmonton: Edmonton Art Gallery, 1980).

———. *La société d'art contemporain, Montréal, 1939–1948* (Edmonton : Edmonton Art Gallery, 1980).

James Edward Hervey (J.E.H.) MacDonald

Duval, Paul. *The Tangled Garden: The Art of J.E.H. MacDonald* (Scarborough, ON: Prentice-Hall, 1978).

Hill, Charles C. *Exploring the Collections: Bouquets from a Tangled Garden* (Ottawa: National Gallery of Canada, 1975).

Edward Middleton Manigault

Beth A. Venn. *Edward Middleton Manigault: His Life and Work* (Master's Thesis, University of Delaware, 1998).

David Milne

Milne, David, Jr., and David P. Silcox. *David B. Milne: Catalogue Raisonné of the Paintings*, 2 vols. (Toronto: University of Toronto, 1998).

O'Brian, John. *David Milne and the Modern Tradition of Painting* (Toronto: Coach House Press, 1983).

———. *David Milne: The New York Years 1903–1916* (Edmonton: Edmonton Art Gallery, 1981).

———. "James Wilson Morrice: His Relationship with the Avant-Garde in France," *O Kanada* (Ottawa: Canada Council, 1985), pp. 57–62.

———. "Morrice – O'Conor, Gauguin, Bonnard et Vuillard," *Revue de l'université de Moncton* 15 (April–December / avril–décembre 1982), p. 9–34.

Silcox, David P. *Painting Place: The Life and Work of David B. Milne* (Toronto: University of Toronto Press, 1996).

James Wilson Morrice

Cloutier, Nicole, et al. *James Wilson Morrice 1865–1924* (Montreal: Montreal Museum of Fine Arts, 1985).

Hill, Charles C. *Morrice. Gift to the Nation: The Collection of G. Blair Laing* (Ottawa: National Gallery of Canada, 1992).

O'Brian, John. "Morrice – O'Conor, Gauguin, Bonnard et Vuillard," *Revue de l'Université de Moncton* 15 (April–December / avril–décembre 1982), p. 9–34.

Le Nigog

Roquebrune, Robert de. *Cherchant mes Souvenirs, 1911–1940* (Montréal/Paris : Fides, 1968).

Trépanier, E. "Un *nigog* lancé dans la mare des arts plastiques," *Archives des lettres canadiennes* 7 (Montréal : Fides, 1987), p. 239–267.

Albert Henry Robinson

Watson, Jennifer. *Albert H. Robinson: The Mature Years* (Kitchener, ON: Kitchener-Waterloo Art Gallery, 1982).

Anne Savage

Anne Savage Archives, Department of Art Education and Art Therapy, Faculty of Fine Arts, Concordia University, Montreal (Leah Sherman [Finding Aid], *Anne Savage Archives*, 1896–1971, Montreal: Concordia University, 1989, unpublished).

Braide, Janet. *Anne Savage: Her Expression of Beauty* (Montreal: Montreal Museum of Fine Art, 1979).

McDougall, Anne. *Anne Savage: The Story of a Canadian Painter* (Montreal: Harvest House, 1977).

Sherman, Leah. *Anne Savage: A Retrospective* (Montreal: Sir George Williams University, 1969).

———. "Anne Savage: A Study of her Development as an Artist / Teacher in the Canadian Art World, 1925-1950," in David Thistlewood (ed.), *Histories of Art and Design Education* (Harlow, Essex: Longman in association with the National Society for Education in Art and Design, 1992), pp. 142–151.

Tom Thomson

Murray, Joan. *Tom Thomson: Design for a Canadian Hero* (Toronto: Dundurn Press, 1998).

———. *Tom Thomson: Trees* (Toronto: McArthur & Co., 1999).

Illustration Credits / Crédits photographiques

Arnot Art Museum, Elmira, New York: 105

Art Gallery of Hamilton: 53, 59, 76, 109, 120, 131

Art Gallery of Ontario / Musée des beaux-arts de l'Ontario, Toronto: 79, 94, 98

Marjorie Lismer Bridges, Ashton, Maryland: 81

Canadian Centre for Architecture / Centre canadien d'architecture, Fonds Ernest Cormier, Montréal, 001-ARC-496: 68 (det.)

Columbus Museum of Art, Ohio: 104

Concordia University / Université Concordia, Montréal, Anne Savage Papers: 129

Edmonton Art Gallery (Harry Korol): 82

Dr. Naomi Jackson Groves, Ottawa: 78 (det.)

Macdonald Stewart Art Centre, University of Guelph: 140

McMichael Canadian Art Collection / Collection McMichael d'art canadien, Kleinburg: 46, 52, 64, 72, 112, 114, 135, 137

Montreal Museum of Fine Arts / Musée des beaux-arts de Montréal: 117, 121–123

Musée du Québec: 25, 86, (Jean-Guy Kérouac) 88, (Patrick Altman) 127

Museum London: 93, (Edward Manigault Collection) 102 (det.), 115

Dr. Sean B. Murphy, Montreal: 42

National Archives of Canada / Archives nationales du Canada, Ottawa: (C57194) 111 (det.), (PA125406) 133 (det.)

National Gallery of Canada / Musée des beaux-arts du Canada, Ottawa: 43, 50, 58, 61 (det.), 69, 71 (det.), 75 (det.), 78 (det.), 87, 91, 96, 108, 126, 130

Photo Archives Matisse, Paris: 13, 84 (det.)

Private collections: 45 (det.), 54, 65, 73, 92, 113, 136, 138–139

The Robert McLaughlin Gallery, Oshawa (Thomas Moore): 47, 99–100, 119

University College Art Collection, University of Toronto: 48, 63

Acknowledgements

In preparing this text, I have been greatly helped by curators, registrars, cataloguers, collectors and art educators. I would like to thank the following individuals and public and private galleries in particular for their help with information, the location of works and supplying photographs: Christine Braun of the Art Gallery of Hamilton; Randall Speller of the Edward P. Taylor Library of the Art Gallery of Ontario, Toronto; Laura Brandon of the Canadian War Museum, Ottawa; D.B.G. Fair of the Museum London; Cathy Mastin of the Glenbow Museum in Calgary; Barbara Meadowcroft, Sandy Cooke and Linda Tanake of the McMichael Canadian Art Collection in Kleinburg; Jean Pierre Labiau and Thérèse Bourgault of the Montreal Museum of Fine Arts; Michèle Grandbois, Elise Bélanger and Nicole Gastonguay at the Musée du Québec; Maija Vilcins at the National Gallery of Canada, Ottawa; Ash Prakash in Toronto; Leah Sherman in Montreal; and Patricia Bovey and Anneke Shea Harrison of the Winnipeg Art Gallery. In The Robert McLaughlin Gallery in Oshawa, where I am director emerita, I'd like to thank David Aurandt, Pat Claxton-Oldfield, Linda Jansma, Melanie Johnston and many other staff members who generously offered assistance. I thank them for their help. I would also like to thank Liz Wylie of the University of Toronto Art Centre, Charles C. Hill of the National Gallery of Canada, Jeremy Brown and Russell Bingham who kindly offered suggestions about the catalogue text.

Among the donors to the show, I would particularly like to mention Bruce Smith, who started the show on its way.

Joan Murray, Oshawa

Remerciements

La préparation de ce texte a été rendue possible grâce à la collaboration de conservateurs, d'archivistes, d'experts en préparation de catalogue, de collectionneurs et de professeurs d'art. Je tiens à leur exprimer ma profonde reconnaissance. Des remerciements particuliers vont aux personnes ainsi qu'aux galeries publiques et privées suivantes, pour leur assistance en matière de renseignements, de recherche d'œuvres et de procuration de photographies: Christine Braun de l'Art Gallery of Hamilton; Randall Speller de l'Edward P. Taylor Library du Musée des beaux-arts de l'Ontario, Toronto; Laura Brandon du Canadian War Museum, Ottawa; D.B.G. Fair du Museum London; Cathy Mastin du Glenbow Museum, Calgary ; Barbara Meadowcroft, Sandy Cooke et Linda Tanake de la Collection McMichael d'art canadien, Kleinburg; Jean-Pierre Labiau et Thérèse Bourgault du Musée des beaux-arts de Montréal; Michèle Grandbois, Elise Bélanger et Nicole Gastonguay du Musée du Québec; Maija Vilcins du Musée des beaux-arts du Canada, Ottawa; Ash Prakash de Toronto et Leah Sherman de Montréal; et Patricia Bovey et Anneke Shea Harrison de la Winnipeg Art Gallery. À la galerie dont je suis directrice émérite, The Robert McLaughlin Gallery à Oshawa, j'ai bénéficié de l'aide de David Aurandt, Pat Claxton-Oldfield, Linda Jansma, Melanie Johnston et d'un nombre considérable d'autres personnes. Je les remercie chaleureusement pour leur collaboration. J'aimerais aussi témoigner ma gratitude à Liz Wylie de l'University of Toronto Art Centre, Charles C. Hill du Musée des beaux-arts du Canada, et à Jeremy Brown et Russell Bingham pour leur suggestions concernant le texte du catalogue.

Enfin, parmi les donateurs et donatrices, il faut mentionner Bruce Smith qui a joué un rôle-clef dans la mise en branle de cette exposition.

Joan Murray, Oshawa